Daily life at the time of Jesus

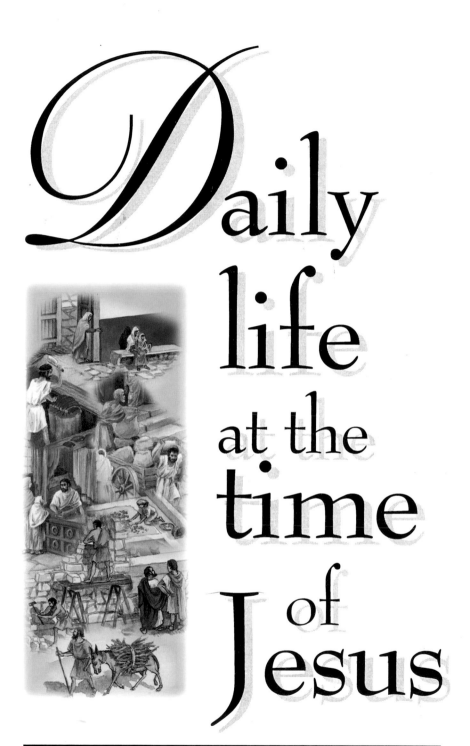

Contents

Introduction

In today's world, many seek knowledge about places, peoples and cultures in far-away corners of the planet. Yet within reach of our hand is one "far-away culture" that should beckon to us more than any other. The characters that people this place, though it has all but vanished in the ordinary sense, are as real to us as our friends and neighbors. They are there to greet us, larger than life, whenever we open our Bible. If we seek to understand the world around us, even the remotest of places we may never visit, how much more do we need to forge a link with the world and the people of the Bible, from which we draw both life lessons and spiritual strength!

In order to truly comprehend the message of Jesus we must understand the cultural background in which that message was forged. That is the task of this book. It seeks to bridge the multi-millennial divide that separates us from the culture of Jesus' day, and to make that culture accessible to all.

The book introduces the reader to these all-important people and the minutiae of their lives in the most natural way possible: it starts with the "macro"—bringing you into a village or a city from the time of Jesus — and progresses to the "micro", moving from the street into the home, workshop, synagogue or market place, as it looked in Jesus' time. You will meet the lord of a Galilee manor and his wife, tour his farm and even get a glimpse of the family tomb. Jerusalem will come alive as you join pilgrims on their way to the Temple. And much, much more.

Tantalizing traces of the age of Jesus are still visible through the twin disciplines of history and archaeology. The numerous New Testament quotations in the book demonstrate that the Gospels remain the most significant of sources for many aspects of daily life in the time of Jesus. As a historical source we also turned to Jewish revolutionary commander-turned imperial historian Josephus Flavius, who has left us a contemporary account of many events of the period. In spite (or perhaps because) of enduring scholarly debate over some of his statements, his works are of paramount importance in the historiography of the period. And the Talmud, especially its early component, the Mishnah (a collection of teachings of Jewish sages compiled in Palestine around 200 CE), although it was set down in writing beginning more than a century after Jesus, is an invaluable reference when fleshing out the details of everyday life of the people among whom Jesus lived.

Last but not least, archaeology brings everything together. Imagine holding a tool in your hand, a tool that was last touched by a human hand some twenty centuries ago, perhaps even by someone who saw Jesus with his or her own eyes. While archaeological evidence is of course open to interpretation, such evidence has been called upon regularly to help bring alive many of the elements of the immortal story told in the New Testament.

It is our hope that you will find this book worthy of its goal and purpose — to bring you as close as possible to life as it was lived in the days of Jesus.

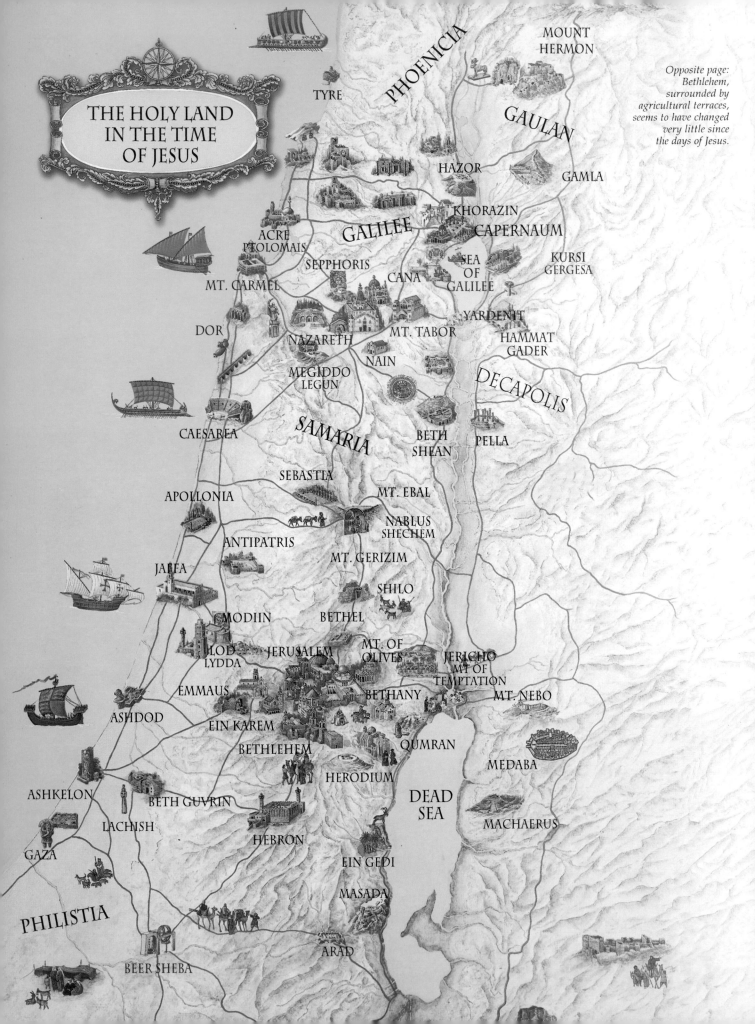

THE HOLY LAND
IN THE TIME
OF JESUS

PHOENICIA

MOUNT
HERMON

GAULAN

Opposite page:
Bethlehem,
surrounded by
agricultural terraces,
seems to have changed
very little since
the days of Jesus.

TYRE

HAZOR

GAMLA

KHORAZIN

GALILEE

CAPERNAUM

ACRE
PTOLOMAIS

SEPPHORIS

CANA

SEA
OF
GALILEE

KURSI
GERGESA

MT. CARMEL

DOR

NAZARETH

MT. TABOR

YARDENIT

HAMMAT
GADER

NAIN

MEGIDDO
LEGUN

DECAPOLIS

CAESAREA

SAMARIA

BETH
SHEAN

PELLA

SEBASTIA

APOLLONIA

MT. EBAL

ANTIPATRIS

NABLUS
SHECHEM

JAFFA

MT. GERIZIM

SHILO

MODIN

BETHEL

LOD
LYDDA

JERUSALEM

MT. OF
OLIVES

JERICHO
MT OF
TEMPTATION

EMMAUS

BETHANY

MT. NEBO

ASHDOD

EIN KAREM

QUMRAN

BETHLEHEM

MEDABA

HERODIUM

ASHKELON

BETH GUVRIN

DEAD
SEA

LACHISH

MACHAERUS

GAZA

HEBRON

EIN GEDI

MASADA

PHILISTIA

ARAD

BEER SHEBA

Seven-branched candelabrum from a first century home in Jerusalem

When Worlds Collide

Times and Signs

"**B**ut when Herod was dead, behold, an angel of the Lord appeared in a dream to Joseph in Egypt, saying, "Arise, take the young child and his mother, and go to the land of Israel, for those who sought the young child's life are dead"... But when he heard that Archelaus was reigning over Judea instead of his father Herod, he was afraid to go there. And being warned by God in a dream, he turned aside into the region of Galilee. And he came and dwelt in a city called Nazareth... In those days, John the Baptist came preaching in the wilderness of Judea and saying "Repent, for the kingdom of heaven is at hand." (Matt 2:19-3:2)

In about 4 BCE, Jesus, Joseph and Mary returned from Egypt to the Holy Land from whence they had fled to escape the murderous rampage of Herod the Great as he sought out the King of the Jews he had been told had been born in Bethlehem.

It was not the first time the Jewish population of the Holy Land found itself the object of cruel and oppressive tactics at the hand of their rulers. But no matter how harsh times were, their faith told them that the days of the Romans were numbered. Inspired by the prophets of old, the Jews fervently awaited the appearance of their Messiah. That day would signal the end of the earthly domination of despots, and God's holy habitation, the Temple in Jerusalem, would be liberated both from foreign rule and local corruption.

Coin of Hasmonean King Alexander Janaeus (103-76 BCE)

In this unswerving belief, the Jews were unlike any of the numerous other peoples ingested by the voracious Empire on the Tiber, peoples whose deities could somehow always be made to blend with those of the Roman pantheon. The God of the Jews—the one, invisible, omnipotent master of the universe, could never be worshipped alongside a mere idol of stone.

Yet Rome persisted in its efforts to force the Jews into the Roman mold. Using Jewish rulers, it attempted to imitate precisely the kind of dominion that it executed successfully in other areas of the empire. But in the Holy Land, each step taken by the conquerors and their local surrogates brought not the peace and quiet that Rome needed to govern; rather, it brought cultural, political and religious life ever closer to chaos.

The signs were all there, it was whispered in the market place and the field, around many a family table, and even in the Temple courts itself—the reign of justice by the long-awaited king-messiah could not be far off.

Before the Romans

Rome had not always ruled Judea directly as it began to do shortly after the family of Jesus came to live in Nazareth. True, Rome's presence had long been felt in the region—it had first made itself known to the Maccabees, the founding fathers of the Hasmonean dynasty of Jewish priest-rulers of the second and early first century BCE, making pacts with them to form a united front against their common enemy, the Selucids. But at that time, Rome desired no more than a cursory connection to the small country with its odd provincial religion.

Oil lamps

But in the middle of the first century BCE, Antipater II, the father of Herod the Great, had his own agenda with the Romans. He sought in the Romans the powerful allies he needed in order to maintain his hold over huge tracts of land and vast assets, obtained during the rule of his own father, Antipater I. A nobleman from Idumea, which was located south and east of Judea (and

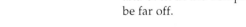

Herod born	Hasmonean Queen Alexandra dies	Pompey captures Jerusalem	Antipater, Herod's father, appointed ruler of Judea
73 BCE	67 BCE	63 BCE	62 BCE

6

known in the Bible as Edom), Antipater I had first begun to amass that wealth as he gradually ingratiated himself with the Hasmoneans, who had conquered his homeland and eventually appointed him its governor.

Now events in the Hasmonean family would draw the Romans into the Judean arena. The military and political policies of one of the most famous of the Hasmonean kings, Alexander Janaeus (103-76 BCE), made him many enemies. Among them were the Pharisees, Bible teachers and sages who disparaged the hellenized ways of the court and the king's ties with their aristocratic opponents, the Sadducees. But Alexander's deathbed wish was for his wife Alexandra to effect a reconciliation with the Pharisees, and during her nine-year reign this policy shift led to some semblance of unity and order.

When Alexandra died in 67 BCE, civil war erupted as her two sons, Hyrcanus and Aristobulus, vied for the office of high priest. Whoever held this office controlled the interests of the Hasmonean ruling house with its vast land holdings. In addition, the high priest oversaw all aspects of Temple worship and administration and many aspects of civil administration as well.

As custom dictated, Hyrcanus, the elder of the two brothers, became high priest. But Hyrcanus was weak and his brother Aristobulus, backed by the Sadducees (who sought to regain influence lost during the period of royal reconciliation with the Pharisees), did all he could to depose him. Wily old Antipater backed Hyrcanus precisely because his weakness made him easier to control.

The Romans understood that these squabbles on the fringes of their empire could have dire effects for them unless they intervened. They had an enemy in the neighborhood: Tigranes, King of Armenia, who had crept down towards Syria and reached as far as Acre in the north of Israel, without opposition. Queen Alexandra had even placated him with gifts.

The High Priest, from a 17th century map by J.F. Bernard

Nabatean tomb at Petra

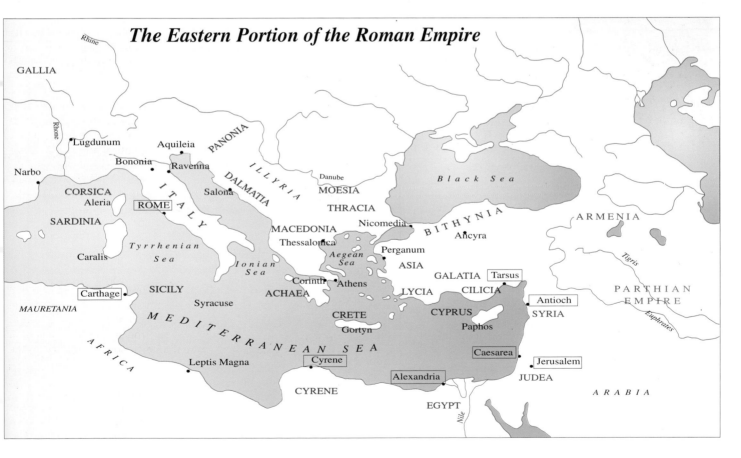

The Eastern Portion of the Roman Empire

[Map showing: GALLIA, Rhine, Rhone, Lugdunum, Narbo, Aquileia, Bononia, Ravenna, PANONIA, ILLYRIA, DALMATIA, Salona, MOESIA, Danube, THRACIA, Black Sea, CORSICA, Aleria, ITALY, ROME, MACEDONIA, Thessalonica, Nicomedia, BITHYNIA, Ancyra, ARMENIA, SARDINIA, Tyrrhenian Sea, Caralis, Ionian Sea, Aegean Sea, Perganum, ASIA, GALATIA, Tarsus, Tigris, PARTHIAN EMPIRE, Corinth, Athens, LYCIA, CILICIA, Carthage, SICILY, ACHAEA, Antioch, Syracuse, CRETE, CYPRUS, SYRIA, Euphrates, MAURETANIA, MEDITERRANEAN SEA, Gortyn, Paphos, AFRICA, Leptis Magna, Cyrene, Caesarea, Jerusalem, Alexandria, JUDEA, ARABIA, CYRENE, EGYPT, Nile]

Gabinius, governor of Syria, quells Judean revolt

Crassus succeeds Gabinius, robs the Jerusalem Temple

Caesar crosses the Rubicon to defeat Pompey

Antipater appoints his son Phasael governor of Jerusalem and his son Herod governor of Galilee

57 BCE   54 BCE   49 BCE   47 BCE

Acre, known in Jesus' day as Ptolemais (Acts 21: 7)

Rome did not approve. It struck at Syria, snatching it away from the clutches of the Armenian king. With this action, Rome was now at the gates of the Holy Land. It was the weak brother Hyrcanus, whining to the Romans of his difficulties in maintaining control of his people, who opened the gates, and out-of-power Aristobulus who beckoned them inward.

Rome, Master of Jerusalem

Aristobulus had persuaded his brother to change places with him and thus he took over the office of high priest. Antipater, from the safety of Idumea, warned Hyrcanus that this was only a first step before Aristobulus eventually did away with him. He convinced Hyrcanus to join him and his old allies the Nabateans in attacking Aristobulus, and they besieged the Temple. Together with his Sadducean confederates, Aristobulus barricaded himself behind its fortress-like walls and a standoff ensued.

Hyrcanus called upon the Romans to aid him against Aristobulus. Rome, whose priority was to end the siege that was depleting the resources of her Nabatean client-kingdom, ordered King Aretas of the Nabateans to head for home.

The Hyrcania Fortress, one of Herod's stronghold-palaces

The siege was lifted. Aristobulus fled to Alexandrion, a Hasmonean fortress in the Jordan Valley, with General Pompey in hot pursuit. Clearly, the Romans had won, or so they thought. But when Pompey's second-in-command, Gabinius, arrived at the Temple gates, he was refused entrance! It was Pompey's turn to mount a siege and in 63 BCE he conquered Jerusalem. Thousands were massacred in the ensuing takeover.

Now that Rome was in charge, the next step was to instill the domestic tranquility without which Rome's interests could not be advanced. Pompey divided Rome's newest possession into administrative regions consisting of Judea, Samaria, Galilee and Peraea, east of the River Jordan. Hyrcanus was awarded a truncated kingdom, and he saw the vast lands his Maccabean forefathers had once brought under Jewish control returned to their former pagan masters.

But things refused to calm down; though Aristobulus had been neutralized — imprisoned in Rome by Pompey — his son Alexander started a guerrilla war against his uncle Hyrcanus. And so Gabinius, instead of resting on his laurels, had to use up Rome's resources to defeat the insurgents. His Roman masters never forgave him for being unable to instill law and order more quickly. Gabinius ended his Palestinian career in exile.

Trouble in Rome

Rome itself now experienced one of its many fateful upheavals. The famed Triumvirate, consisting of Pompey, Julius Caesar and Crassus, was about to fall apart. In 53 BCE, Crassus died fighting against the Parthian Empire on the banks of the Euphrates. Julius Caesar and Pompey faced off against each other. Caesar crossed the Rubicon River near Ravenna in Italy to meet his rival, emerged triumphant, and the future of Judea was transformed.

Marble bust of Pompey

Aristobulus, whose anger against Pompey had been nurtured during long years in prison, threw in his lot with Julius Caesar, who liberated him. Caesar even promised Aristobulus two legions with which to go to Judea and restore his holdings. But before he could leave Rome, agents loyal to Pompey poisoned him. His son Alexander, too, was killed.

Meanwhile, Antipater had prudently also transferred his loyalty from Pompey to Caesar. Soon enough the opportunity arose for him to prove his change of heart: after Crassus' defeat at the hands of the Parthians, Galiliean revolutionaries took advantage of the temporary loosening of Rome's control to try to throw off the yoke of the conqueror altogether. Antipater helped quell this revolt. He also advised Hyrcanus to encourage the Jews of Egypt to support Caesar. Their positive influence helped pave the way to Caesar's becoming master of the Nile.

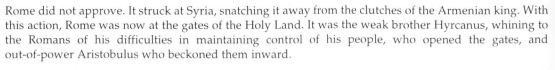

Antigonus appointed high priest and king — 40 BCE

Herod becomes King of Judea — 37 BCE

Antony loses the battle of Actium to Octavian — 31 BCE

Herod executes High Priest Hyrcanus — 30 BCE

Reign of Augustus — **30 BCE-14 CE**

In thanks to Antipater, Caesar declared the high priesthood hereditary in Hyrcanus' line. Now Antipater finally began to reap the fruits of his labors. Caesar appointed him procurator of Judea, which had become a subdivision of the larger Roman province of Syria. As his title indicated, Antipater was in charge of "procuring" all of Rome's needs. With all the tax monies of the region, as well as the revenues of Hyrcanus' abundant private properties at his disposal, Antipater was as rich and powerful as he ever dreamed of being.

In the ensuing years, Hyrcanus fell so far under the influence of Antipater that he allowed the shrewd old Idumean to appoint his own eldest son Phasael to the office of Prefect, or governor, of Jerusalem. At this time another son of Antipater appeared on the scene. During the wars of succession between Hyrcanus and Aristobulus, this son of Antipater, ten years old at the time, had been dispatched home to Idumea for safekeeping. Now he was sent for, and at 26 years old found himself governor of Galilee. His name was Herod.

"The Rulers of the Gentiles..."

"... the rulers of the Gentiles lord it over them, and those who are great exercise authority over them. Yet it shall not be so among you..." (Matt 20:25-26)

The Wealth of Herod

According to one estimate, Herod's yearly income was at least 13 million denarii, a sum equal in today's terms to over 1.6 million dollars. His wealth accrued from several sources: taxes on agricultural produce, for example, was a fourth, a third on grain, and up to one-half of the yield on fruit. Until Cleopatra took them from him, Herod owned balsam plantations in Jericho and Ein Gedi, manufacturing a perfume from this mysterious plant that was worth its weight in gold. Herod extracted tolls and duties from the caravans bringing spices like frankincense and myrrh from Arabia across his territories to the port in Gaza. Much of the economy of Judea was stimulated by the existence of the Temple. Doves and other animals were raised for sacrifice and sold in the markets of Jerusalem together with incense and all the other items required by visitors and pilgrims. On all these, Herod imposed taxes.

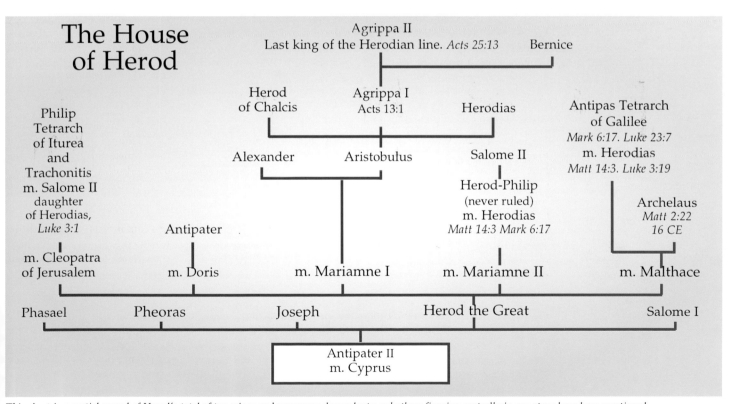

The House of Herod

This chart is a partial record of Herod's total of ten wives and numerous descendants; only those figuring centrally in our story have been mentioned.

Octavian assumes the title Augustus — 27 BCE

Herod builds Caesarea — 22 BCE

Herod builds the Temple — 18 BCE

Quirinius governor of Syria — c.6 BCE

Artist's rendering of the Temple of Augustus in Caesarea

If Herod hoped to wield power as other Roman provincial rulers did, he was soon to discover that Jewish traditions of government complicated his task. Shortly after he assumed his office the young governor found himself summoned before the Sanhedrin, the supreme judicial body of the Jews, after his father's adversaries accused him of illegally executing Hezekias, an insurgent who was terrorizing the region. Herod did appear before the Sanhedrin in Jerusalem but later fled to the Romans, pleading for help against his recalcitrant subjects.

To bolster his case, Herod showered gifts on the Romans. In return they offered him the position of governor of the regions of Coele-Syria (probably biblical Phoenicia) and Samaria, together with palaces, lands and farms. Herod now came to a fateful conclusion: in the future, he realized, his authority would depend not on the devotion of his Jewish subjects, but on the whim of his Roman overlords.

Once again, events in Rome took a turn that would affect the tiny Judean kingdom. In 44 BCE Julius Caesar was murdered by Brutus and Cassius. Ascendant now were Mark Antony and Octavian, Julius Caesar's nephew. One prominent victim of this upheaval was Herod's father Antipater, poisoned by one of his many enemies at a feast.

It was now time for Jerusalem to pay obeisance to the newest of Rome's rulers. Together with Herod and Phasael, Hyrcanus traveled to Antioch where Antony was holding court. On that occasion, Antony, anxious for the supplies Herod could procure for him, confirmed the rule of the young governor. Hyrcanus remained ethnarch (ruler of the nation) but now, thanks to Mark Antony, both Herod and his brother Phasael held the title of tetrarchs, or regional rulers for Rome.

Herod's Fractious Kingdom

When Herod assumed power, a volatile fusion of forces unique to Judea tested the firmness of his grasp. Years later, when Judea revolted against Rome, these same forces would be unleashed with a vengeance, changing forever the face of Jewish life and culture.

Many factors have been cited as contributing to the unrest and eventual revolt in Judea. They include Rome's inability to understand its Jewish subjects and the special requirements of the Jewish faith, the cruelty of Rome's rule, and the close physical proximity and resulting friction between Jewish and pagan communities in various locations of Palestine. In the century following the revolt and destruction of the Temple, Jewish sages added their own *causus belli*: they ascribed the destruction of the Temple to baseless hatred between Jews, a motif that recurs frequently in Jewish literature down through the ages.

Roman troops

Seeds of revolt were planted in soil no doubt fertilized also by a power struggle within the Jewish ruling class. Central to this indigenous ruling class was the priesthood. When the Romans took Jerusalem in 63 BCE, it was ostensibly to restore the High Priest Hyrcanus to power as ruler of the people. But what kind of ruler was he? Not the regal priest the people expected of the offspring of their heroic Judah the Maccabee, one who would make bold political and military decisions and safeguard the purity of their holy Temple. Sadly, Hyrcanus was no more than a feeble version of those kings of old, and he commanded little support among the people.

Herod, whose family had been converted to Judaism during the territorial conquests of Hasmonean King John Hyrcanus (134-104 BCE), also had no inherent legitimacy in the eyes of the people, and maintained his power thanks mainly to Roman intervention. Among his many excesses, in the process of ensuring that power, Herod had ordered the execution of most members of the Jewish aristocracy who had supported Aristobulus.

The Antonia Fortress at the Holyland Model of Second Temple-era Jerusalem

Herod's most famous attempt to curry favor with the Jewish ruling class was his marriage to the Hasmonean princess Mariamne. His continued efforts to create a ruling class loyal to him included awarding lands and possessions to a succession of minor nobles and anonymous landowners. Among them was the father of the second Mariamne (another Hasmonean noblewoman with whom Herod became enamored and married after his execution of the first Mariamne), whom Herod had made high priest. This class of nobles who owed their standing to Herod were the "herodians" mentioned in Matthew 22:16, Mark 3:6 and Mark 12:13.

Birth of Jesus		Death of Herod			Archelaus banished
c. 6-4 BCE		c. 4 BCE		BCE/CE	6 CE

Wealthy men were a familiar sight in both Judea and Galilee, as numerous New Testament references affirm (Matt 9:35-38, Matt 13:24-27, Matt 13:44, Matt 18:23-34). Among the wealthy were local administrators like Chuza, "Herod's steward" (Luke 8:3), whose wife Joanna became a disciple of Jesus and helped support him. Wealth was primarily linked to land ownership, with land often acquired by buying up property from people who defaulted on loans during bad harvests or all-too-frequent droughts. Many such people deprived of their land joined the ranks of the "robbers" or "bandits" often referred to by Josephus. But to the simple folk, these people were heroes, as they refused to bow down to Rome's rule or that of its wealthy proxies. Scholars believe that Barabbas, the "robber" of John 18:40, could have been one of these insurgents.

Leptons, or "widows' mites".

Herod's policies regarding the priesthood also led to friction. He took drastic steps to keep the high priesthood under his thumb, among which was the humiliating confiscation of their sacred vestments which he ordered stored in the Antonia Fortress. His constant clashes with the priesthood left him with at least one group of strange bed-fellows, the Essenes, anchorites who also opposed the high priest, albeit for very different reasons.

The New Testament's frequent pairing of the words "tax collectors" with "sinners" (Matt 9:10, Matt 9:11, Mark 2:16, Luke 5:30, Luke 7:34 *inter alia*) shows that this was a class within the Jewish world of Jesus' day that stirred up the anger of the people. Resistance to tax collectors was not based merely on economic issues. In fact, tax collection, including the Temple tax, seems to have been accepted as long as collectors did not cheat (Luke 3:13). And in other parts of the Roman world, it was precisely the tax collector, seen as a successful local administrator, who rose to prominence. But in Jewish society, tax collectors and other aristocrats were viewed as having attained power without fulfilling the traditional Jewish requirements of good birth and/or Torah learning. Jewish faith and culture taught that it was the "teacher of Israel" (John 3:10) who was to command more respect than any other segment of society.

Herod's northern palace at Masada

With no traditional ruling class in the land, this new group, the teachers, well versed in Torah, attained a measure of authority. Among such people were members of the "local councils", mentioned in Matt 10:17, as well as the rulers of the synagogues (Mark 5:36, Luke 13:14). Scribes (Luke 22:66), their literacy a significant advantage, also wielded power among the people. But they had no standing with the Romans and could not be utilized as the Romans expected of people of status in other provinces, as a line of communication between the people and the imperial powers.

Thus over the course of a century, economic, social and cultural disparities continued to weaken the foundations of society. Storms became tempests; eventually Herod's descendants could no longer weather them and their battered house crashed down around them.

Herod Survives Another Crisis

But at this time, 40 BCE, Herod's star was still on the rise. The renewed attack of an old enemy of Rome, the Parthian Empire, presented him with the opportunity to shine more brightly than ever. With Antony enthralled with Cleopatra, the Parthians had decided to move in on Syria and Lebanon. Antony's dalliance also allowed for agitation to stir in Palestine: Antigonus, son of Aristobulus, still sought to avenge the disgrace of his father who had lost power to Hyrcanus. Antigonus made a pact with the Parthian king, promising him a thousand talents (a huge sum, almost twice what Judea paid Rome in yearly taxes!) and five hundred women if he would help him secure the throne of Jerusalem and kill Herod into the bargain. Invading Judea, Antigonus took the Temple Mount by storm. The Parthians kept up their end of the deal, defeating the forces of Hyrcanus near Mount Carmel, and joined Antigonus in Jerusalem.

Theater at Sepphoris

Herod marched on Jerusalem, but his forces were not strong enough to take the city back from Antigonus, not during the feast of Pentecost when thousands of pilgrims who sided with Antigonus were present. Herod and his brother Phasael were able only to take the Antonia Fortress, and a standoff ensued. To end it, the Parthians, who had not intended to become embroiled in a civil war, suggested that a treaty be concluded between Antigonus, Herod and Phasael under their auspices. Suspicious, Herod refused to come, but Hyrcanus and Phasael were lured in. They were taken captive and handed over to Antigonus.

Antigonus' anger and hatred of his uncle burned within him at the sight of Hyrcanus. He leaped at him and bit off the man's ears, rendering him ritually unfit for the priesthood. Phasael, humiliated at the circumstances of his capture and the shocking mutilation of Hyrcanus, killed himself.

	Caiphas appointed High Priest	Herod Antipas dedicates Tiberias	Pontius Pilate appointed procurator
Reign of Tiberius			
14 CE **14 CE - 37 CE**	18 CE	20 CE	27 CE

When Herod heard this news, he realized that flight from the Parthians was his only hope. He escaped Jerusalem accompanied by an armed escort and hundreds of servants, together with his mother, his fiancée Mariamne (who was none other than the niece of his enemy Antigonus) and her mother. At one point, the wagon carrying his mother overturned and in a fit of depression, Herod would have fallen upon his own sword, but was restrained by his minions. The sorry caravan struggled on and, leaving his family at Masada, Herod parted from the rest of the company and made for the refuge of the Nabatean kingdom to the east.

Despite large sums paid the Nabatean king by Antipater, the chieftains of this desert kingdom feared Parthian reprisals if they helped Herod and they refused to protect him. So Herod turned to Rome, making a perilous winter sea voyage via Rhodes. Upon his arrival, Antony championed him before the Senate, proposing that this man, their valuable ally against the Parthians, be made King of the Jews.

Herod Takes Back His Kingdom

Herod emerged from his Roman trip with a crown and began the battle to take back his dominion. He routed Antigonus out of Masada, where he had sought refuge. He took the central Galilee town of Sepphoris in the midst of a snowstorm and brutally defeated insurrectionists at the Arbel cliff overlooking the main road connecting central Galilee to the Sea of Galilee and the north. Finally, in the summer of 37 BCE, Herod took Jerusalem and married Mariamne.

Herod's conquest of Jerusalem was followed by the beheading of the aristocratic followers of Antigonus. He then appointed as high priest, in place of Hyrcanus, an unknown member of the priesthood from Babylon, one Hananel. But these steps did nothing to put an end to opposition to his rule. It was five years before quiet finally ensued, with Herod's conquest of the desert fortress of Hyrcania from Antigonus' sister. From then on, to ensure order, Herod stationed a Roman legion near Jerusalem, supporting it out of his own funds.

Herod continued to be a powerful ally to Antony. In 31 BCE, he even sent his own troops to fight with Antony at Actium in western Greece, where Octavian met and vanquished the combined forces of Antony and Cleopatra. Luckily, Herod himself was not at the fateful battle, but was off fighting the Nabateans. Consequently, he could convincingly swear fealty to Octavian, now Emperor Augustus, wisely choosing on that occasion, as a sign of humility, not to wear his crown. Herod showered money and gifts on Augustus, who rewarded him by restoring lands Herod had lost to the machinations of Cleopatra.

Before his rendezvous with the new Emperor, Herod cleaned up the last of his domestic imbroglios. Hyrcanus, the deposed old high priest, still seemed to pose a threat through his daughter Alexandra, mother of Mariamne. A consummate schemer, Alexandra had worked to have Herod's appointee, the anonymous Hananel, deposed in favor of her son Aristobulus II, Mariamne's younger brother. In so doing, though, she unwittingly signed her son's death warrant. When the handsome, seventeen year-old Aristobulus appeared on the Feast of Tabernacles, resplendent in priestly robes, before crowds of adoring pilgrims in the Jerusalem Temple, Herod could not stand it. He secretly ordered the death of Aristobulus, and his henchmen drowned the young man in the swimming pool of Herod's Jericho palace.

Herod now instituted a new law requiring the people to take an oath of goodwill towards him, with those who refused to be severely punished. Only the Essenes, unlikely allies of the king who could not take such an oath out of religious conviction, were exempted from it by royal decree.

Possessed by unrelenting dread of the real or imagined plots hatched against him by the Hasmoneans, Herod sought recourse in the continued murder of his opponents. With the blood of so many on his hands, it is easy to imagine him carrying out the infamous massacre of the children of Bethlehem and its environs upon hearing that a king of the Jews had been born there, an act attributed to him in the Gospel of Luke.

Herod could not have known that at least two children would survive that massacre. Jesus, spirited to Egypt by Joseph, would return to Galilee only after Herod's death and grow to maturity in Nazareth.

The Arbel cliff

The traditional grotto, home of Joseph and Mary in Nazareth

"The Flight to Egypt" as shown in a contemporary Bethlehem church

John the Baptist beheaded	Jesus crucified	Death of Philip the Tetrarch	Josephus born in Jerusalem	
				Reign of Caligula
c. 28 CE	30 CE	34 CE	37 CE	37 CE - 41 CE

12

Another child, legend relates, survived the massacre when his mother concealed him in a cave. And that child, John, would grow up to baptize many in the River Jordan, preaching the end of days and the coming of a savior.

After his confirmation by Emperor Augustus, Herod sent for his two sons by Mariamne, Alexander and Aristobulus, who had been educated in Rome. But Herod's sister, their aunt Salome, viewed them as rivals and began to plot against them. Antipater, Herod's son by his first wife Doris, joined the cabal. Rumors reached Augustus, in whose court Alexander and Aristobulus had been raised. He held the young men in high regard and refused to believe the slander. The Emperor summoned the unhappy family to Rome for an audience. They returned to Jerusalem chastised, but only barely reconciled.

The Jordan River

The Unraveling

When Herod returned to Judea from his dressing-down by Augustus, he announced the line of succession: first would be Antipater, his eldest son, after him Alexander and finally Aristobulus. But amidst unremitting accusations and counteraccusations, things began to fall apart. Herod made some calamitous political blunders at this time too, among them his refusal to allow his sister Salome to marry Syllaeus, a Nabatean noble (Herod had never forgiven the Nabateans for not protecting him). The spurned nobleman stirred up trouble against Herod in Trachonitis, east of the Jordan, one of Herod's principalities. When rebels from that region fled to Arabia, Herod pursued and massacred them. Augustus was so furious at Herod's incursion onto foreign soil that he refused to even see his protégé. Reduced now by a paranoid fear of everyone who surrounded him, Herod ordered the execution of Mariamne and of her mother Alexandra.

Intrigue followed upon intrigue and fabricated evidence continued to pile up against Aristobulus and Alexander. Augustus now allowed Herod to call upon the king of Syria to act as an arbitrator in this venomous family feud. A tribunal, packed with Herod's own supporters, condemned the princes to death. "It is better to be Herod's pig than Herod's son," Augustus is reputed to have said in the wake of this action. At this time too, Herod's own army, within whose ranks were many supporters of Aristobulus and Alexander, began to murmur against their king.

Antipater was only briefly secure in his position as heir apparent. For soon the erratic Herod decided to make amends for the murder of his sons by seeing to the future of his now orphaned grandchildren by marrying them off to each other and making other family members their guardians. Antipater dealt with this threat by hatching a plot together with his uncle, Herod's brother Pheoras, to poison the king.

Herod's sister Salome, ever with her ear to the palace walls, reported the plot to Herod, who had Pheoras' servants tortured until they revealed the truth. Herod now ordered the execution of Antipater (Although receiving permission from Augustus to carry it out, it was not implemented immediately). He changed his will so that now succession passed to Antipas, his youngest son by the Samaritan queen Malthace.

Herodium, between Bethlehem and the Judean wilderness

Life at court was noxious; new plots were hatched behind every door. And Herod, now about seventy years of age, was riddled with ailments of all kinds, a fact that was noised abroad by enemy agents in the palace.

Encouraged by the thought that the maniacal despot was not long for this world, two young and influential sages in Jerusalem let it be known that the time was ripe to pull down the hated golden eagle that Herod had ordered placed above the great gate of the Temple in honor of Rome. In broad daylight, in front of the crowds, the eagle was pulled to the ground. The young men were caught and brought before the king, who roused himself from his sickbed to interrogate them personally, after which he ordered them burned alive. Now Herod's sickness, whose symptoms have been interpreted variously as liver failure, intestinal cancer or syphilis, took him over entirely. He retired for treatment to Callirhoe, famed cascading hot springs east of the Dead Sea.

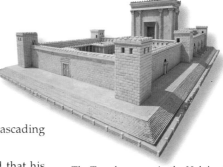

The Temple as seen in the Holyland Model of Second Temple-era Jerusalem

Typical of Herod was the order he gave as he lay dying in his palace in Jericho. He demanded that his sister Salome incarcerate the most important leaders of the Jews, with orders to slay them when news

	Death of Agrippa I	Paul's first missionary journey	Agrippa II assumes power	Felix procurator of Judea
Reign of Claudius				
41 CE	**41 CE - 54 CE** 44 CE	45 CE	48 CE	52 CE

came of the King's death. The goal of this action? To ensure that the Jewish people would have reason to mourn when the King died.

From his jail cell, the condemned Antipater, too, heard about Herod's impending death, and now attempted to bribe his jailers to release him. Herod's wrath upon hearing this was rekindled, and he ordered the sentence of execution against Antipater carried out. He then changed his will once more making another son by Malthace, Archelaus, his successor. To Antipas, he awarded Peraea and Galilee while his son Philip (by the fifth of Herod's ten wives, Cleopatra of Jerusalem) received the upper Galilee and parts of Syria (Luke 3:1). Herod's scheming sister Salome received huge tracts of land in the coastal plain and the Jordan Valley together with a generous allowance.

Five days after the execution of Antipater, Herod died. Archelaus gave him a splendid funeral; the king's body was draped in the royal purple, a crown and diadem on his head and scepter in his hand. A large crowd of his relatives and an honor guard in full battle regalia accompanied the bier to its mausoleum in Herodium, south of Bethlehem.

The Reign of the Three Brothers

Jesus was born in Bethlehem on the "seam" between the reign of Herod the Great and his son Archelaus. Matthew 2:22 records that Joseph feared Archelaus. And right he was to be afraid, for Archelaus' reign had begun with a massacre of his subjects. News of Herod's death had stirred hopes of relief for the thousands of pilgrims gathered in Jerusalem for Passover. Archelaus, fearing the outbreak of riots, precipitated that very event when he called out the troops to restrain the people. The streets of Jerusalem ran crimson with the blood of the slain.

Josephus records that in opposition to Jewish law, Archelaus divorced his wife to wed his sister-in-law Glaphyra, the widow of his executed brother Alexander and mother of Alexander's three children. Archelaus also ousted two high priests from office in his attempt to control Temple politics. And so now with Archelaus away in Rome having his appointment confirmed by the Emperor, the country seethed. In Galilee, disturbances were instigated by one Judas whose father, Hezekias, Herod had ordered killed at the beginning of his reign. The unrest was put down with great cruelty by Varus, the governor of Syria, and Jerusalem burned.

A delegation of Jews went to Rome to plead their case before Augustus. (A hint of this incident may be found in Luke 19:11-15, Jesus' parable concerning the king whose subjects hated him). In response, Augustus ordered the kingdom divided as Pompey had done before him. He left Archelaus in charge in Judea, Samaria and Idumea with the title of ethnarch, promising to upgrade him to king if his behavior warranted it.

But soon afterwards, in 6 CE, the Romans stripped Archelaus of his possessions, banished him to Vienna and imposed their direct rule on Judea. Judea became a province ruled by Coponius as procurator, while Quirinius ruled as governor of Syria.

One of the first actions of the new rulers was a census, reminiscent of the one mentioned in the Nativity story that brought Joseph and Mary to Bethlehem. Opposition to the census was fiercest among the Zealots, a revolutionary movement that had its roots in the Golan Heights town of Gamla.

Meanwhile, in the north, Philip ruled long and apparently wisely. He built the city of Caesarea Philippi and expanded Bethsaida, home of Apostles Peter, John, James and Andrew, into a polis — a Greek-style city — renaming it Julias in honor of Augustus Caesar's wife. Philip was considered a friend of the Romans and struck the first Jewish coins depicting Augustus and Tiberius. He died childless in 37 CE and his lands temporarily reverted to direct Roman rule.

Antipas is the Herod most often mentioned in the New Testament. During his reign, John the Baptist began his ministry. Like his brother Philip, Herod Antipas inherited his father's penchant for city

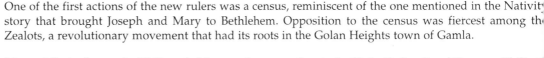

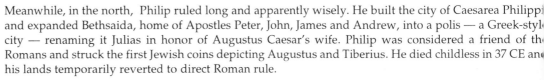

| Paul arrested in Jerusalem | Paul appears before new procurator Festus in Caesarea | Mark's Gospel set down | Great Revolt breaks out | Paul dies in Rome |

Reign of Nero

14 54 CE   **54 CE - 68 CE**   58 CE   60 CE   65 CE   66 CE   68 CE

building. He rebuilt and expanded the city of Sepphoris that had been laid waste during the campaign of Varus and established the city of Tiberias, which he named in honor of the emperor who followed Augustus. The construction of Tiberias was a cause of contention between Antipas and the people, as he transgressed Jewish law by building it on the site of a cemetery.

First married to the daughter of Aretas, Nabatean king of Petra, he then took up with Herodias, the wife of his half-brother Herod-Philip. This action incurred the reproach of John the Baptist (Matthew 14:4, Mark 6:17-18, Luke 3:19) and at the behest of the enticing Salome, Herodias' daughter, Antipas ordered John's execution. Jesus, who famously characterized Herod Antipas as "that fox" (Luke 13:32), eventually met Herod Antipas personally, challenging with silence the Galilean king's attempts to interrogate him (Luke 23:6-12).

In 26 CE, during the reign of Emperor Tiberius, a new procurator took over in Judea, the notorious Pontius Pilate, who judged and condemned Jesus to the cross on the most fateful Passover in history.

Inscription discovered at Caesarea mentioning the name of Pontius Pilate and Emperor Tiberius

Pontius Pilate was hated among the Jews for his attempt to place standards with Roman images in Jerusalem and for robbing the Temple treasury to pay for the construction of an aqueduct. Because of his misdeeds he was ordered to report to the Emperor, but before he could arrive in Rome, Tiberius died and was replaced by the demented Caligula.

Caligula had a friend in Rome, Agrippa, Herod's grandson by his executed son Aristobulus. Agrippa, whose rivalry with Herod Antipas was well-known, had previously been helpless to influence the course of events in Palestine. But now Agrippa saw a chance to step in. He accused Antipas before Caligula of preparing for war against Rome with Parthian assistance. Antipas hurried to Rome to answer Agrippa's accusations of treason but to no avail. His property was confiscated and he lived out his life in exile. Agrippa became king of the northern part of Palestine where Philip had once ruled.

When Caligula was assassinated in 41 CE, Agrippa found himself in Rome during an attempt to calm the latest crisis in his kingdom, precipitated when the mad emperor ordered his statue put up in the Jerusalem Temple. Just in time, Agrippa switched his loyalties to the new Emperor, Claudius.

Acts 12:1-3 records that it was Herod Agrippa who ordered the death of James, the brother of Jesus, and the arrest of Peter. Agrippa's own death, described in Acts as well as by Josephus (Antiquities 19:8:2), was seen as his just deserts: "And upon a set day Herod, arrayed in royal apparel, sat upon his throne, and made an oration unto them. And the people gave a shout, saying, It is the voice of a god, and not of a man. And immediately the angel of the Lord smote him, because he gave not God the glory: and he was eaten of worms, and gave up the ghost" (Acts 12:21-22).

Silver coin of Agrippa I (37-44). Agrippa's father, Aristobulus, riding in a chariot. Above him, written in Greek: "Coin of King Agrippa".

Because his son, Agrippa II, was too young to succeed him at the time, his lands reverted to direct Roman rule. It was the excuse for more Roman mismanagement under the procurator Albinus. Resistance movements such as the Zealots and the Sicarii gained strength during this time.

Jewish rule was restored when Agrippa II assumed the throne in about 50 CE. But Felix, the new Roman overlord, proved incapable of holding together the fabric of society. In fact he encouraged a more rapid rending of its seams: to avenge real or imagined insults, Felix persuaded one of the High Priest Jonathan's friends to bring "robbers"— rebels — upon Jonathan and kill him. Such "robbers", Josephus records, "went up with the greatest security at the festivals after this time, and having weapons concealed ...and mingling themselves among the multitude, they slew certain of their own enemies..."(Antiquities 20:8:3).

The Jews and the gentiles in Caesarea began quarreling over authority in the city, and only the pleading of the Jews themselves before the Roman authorities prevented a massacre by Roman troops. Two factions of the priesthood struggled violently with each other. The Zealots also became uncontrollable, despite the fact that thousands were purged during this time.

The Roman's prize prisoner from the siege of Jotapata was an aristocratic young general named Josephus

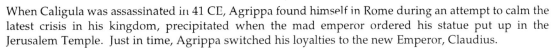

Reigns of Emperors Galba, Otho and Vitellus	Vespasian becomes emperor		Temple is destroyed	Matthew and Luke's Gospel set down	Masada falls
		Reign of Vespasian			
68-69 CE	69 CE	**69 CE - 79 CE**	70 CE	c 70-80 CE	c. 73 CE

Prophyry statue from Caesarea, possibly of Hadrian

The air crackled with political tension. And so, when Paul was seized by Jews from Asia while speaking in the Temple courts, as described in Acts 21, Roman troops jumped into action, racing down from the adjacent Antonia Fortress to arrest him. Interrogating him, the captain of the guard thought he might be the Egyptian who started a revolt and "led four thousand assassins into the desert some time ago" (Acts 21:38). Josephus also makes reference to this messianic figure who had mysteriously disappeared after Felix massacred his followers. Paul was remanded in custody and taken to Roman imperial headquarters in Caesarea. During the two years he spent under house arrest there, Felix was recalled and replaced by Festus.

Festus and Agrippa II found themselves allies in their attempts to maintain order in the dangerously fragmented province. An illustration of their relationship is in the seemingly mundane story recorded by Josephus of a dining room Agrippa built himself with a porch overlooking the Temple. The Jews thought it inappropriate that Agrippa should be able to look into the Temple and so they in their turn built a wall to block his view. Festus ordered the wall pulled down. The Jews sent a petition to Nero in the matter. Nero allowed the Jews to keep the wall, perhaps influenced by his wife Popaea, who, like Cornelius the Caesarean, the nameless Centurion at Capernaum, and no doubt countless other anonymous people, was a righteous Gentile, a god-fearer.

And of course it was Festus and King Agrippa before whom Paul appeared in Caesarea, making his impassioned speech for Christianity recorded in Acts 26. It was also during the reign of King Agrippa that the colossal building project of the Temple came to an end, and eighteen thousand workers suddenly found themselves jobless. This massive unemployment is another factor to which many scholars attribute the imminent outbreak of revolt.

The Temple in Jerusalem as it appeared on a coin issued some 60 years after its destruction during the Bar Kochba Revolt.

66 CE, during the rule of the tyrannical procurator Florus, was the fateful year during which the Great Revolt began. Florus had ordered his soldiers into Jerusalem's Upper City market, plundered it and slain inhabitants of every house. On that day, some 3600 people were flogged and crucified, even, unthinkably, those who were Roman citizens. Riots broke out in Caesarea when gentiles sacrificed a dove in the courtyard of a synagogue. Typically, Florus threw the Jewish community leaders into prison and allowed the Gentile instigators to go unscathed.

Mindful of the watchful and disapproving eye of Rome, Florus did propose a withdrawal of most of his troops from Jerusalem to Caesarea. Agrippa also attempted to calm things down. But it was too little too late. When the people discovered their king's intent was merely to smooth Rome's ruffled feathers until they could replace Florus, they expelled him from Jerusalem.

The next crucial turn towards the point of no return took place when some of the Temple priests were persuaded to reject the Emperor's regular sacrifice, an insult Rome could hardly overlook. Then, in September of 66 CE, Menahem, son of the famous rebel Judas the Galilean (Acts 5:32) took Masada from its Roman guards. He returned to Jerusalem "in the state of a king" (Wars of the Jews 2:17:8) and had the high priest, whose actions he considered too conciliatory towards the Romans, murdered. When Menahem dared to appear in royal robes in the Temple court, supporters of the murdered high priest killed the insurrectionist. But others of Menahem's party escaped to Masada under the leadership of Elazar Ben Ya'ir, a relative of Menahem, to continue the rebellion.

Storage vessels from Masada

Another round of negotiations between the Romans and the Jews ensued during which the Romans gave their adversaries one last chance to surrender. But there was no going back; forces affiliated with the new high priest slaughtered the Romans just as the talks were concluding.

Battles grew more frequent and intense. Cestius Gallus, Roman commander of the Jerusalem front, was defeated by the charismatic rebel leader Simeon Bar Giora in the strategic Bet Horon Pass northwest of the city. Bar Giora, a messianic figure, continued to fight for control of Jerusalem against his rival John of Giscala, right up to the moment of Titus' capture of the city in 70 CE.

Cestius Gallus was replaced in the following year by Vespasian. Together with his son Titus, Vespasian landed at Acre and marched on Galilee expecting a quick victory. But he was mistaken. He was forced to lay siege to the upper Galilee mountain town of Jotapata, which fought bravely for its survival, but finally surrendered.

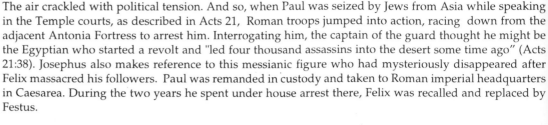

Mount Vesuvius erupts

John's Gospel set down

79 CE

c. 90-100 CE

The Roman's prize prisoner from the siege of Jotapata was an aristocratic young general named Josephus son of Mattathias, who had engineered his own survival from a suicide pact made among the last of the town's defenders. Josephus was taken to Rome where he adopted the Emperor's family name, Flavius. Author of the Wars of the Jews, Antiquities of the Jews and life of Josephus has gone down in history as the chronicler of the revolt he had once led and our only source of information of many of the events of this period.

Head of Titus on gold coin with legend: Imp(erator) Titus Caes(ar) Vespasianus P(ontifex) M(aximus). year 71

Vespasian continued to pursue the war in Galilee, taking the area around the Sea of Galilee, Tiberias, Gamla and finally, Giscala, whose commander John escaped and continued to fight in Jerusalem.

The Fall of Jerusalem

When in 68 CE word of the death of Emperor Nero reached Vespasian, he sent his son Titus together with Agrippa to Rome, to gauge which way the winds of power were blowing. Within the year, in a dizzying succession of events, three more emperors died and troops loyal to Vespasian proclaimed him Emperor. Vespasian departed the Judean battlefield to consolidate his position and Titus was left to pursue the siege of Jerusalem.

Though plagued by internecine warfare, the Jewish defenders of Jerusalem had succeeded thus far in keeping the Roman army at bay. Now Titus surrounded the city on all sides, approaching it from the north where there were no deep valleys to impede his progress. Setting up camp on Mount Scopus, he ordered the defoliation of all the forests around the city and the leveling of all the rocks.

Roman siege machines and huge numbers of soldiers advanced on Jerusalem's walls. At this sight, the two main Jewish factions laid aside their differences and stood upon the wall with torches, running back and forth and shooting arrows at the Romans. Some brave souls sallied out and attacked the siege machines, inflicting whatever damage they could before they were killed. Others set fire to some of the machines. The Roman camp was thrown into a panic and Titus took to encouraging his men by personally making the rounds of the camps and siege towers that surrounded the city. Eventually, the Romans pierced the north wall that had been completed only a few decades before by Agrippa.

Roman siege techniques

Five days later, Jerusalem's older inner wall fell. But the attackers found themselves in dire straits: the city's Jewish inhabitants had a clear advantage in the narrow lanes and markets where the battle now raged. Titus did the best he could to defend his men, running to and fro on the rooftops to snipe at the Jewish fighters with his own weapons.

It was at this point that Titus declared a cease-fire, to give the defenders a chance to consider their situation. Military payday had arrived and Titus used it as an opportunity for another show of strength and to encourage his men. As custom indicated, before receiving their pay the soldiers donned their armor, adorned their horses, and lined up to receive their pay. Large numbers of Jerusalem's citizens watched the curious ceremonies silently from the wall. This activity continued for four days.

Titus then returned to the siege works, now specifically targeting the Antonia Fortress and the Temple beyond. The Jewish defenders constantly found new ways to harass the Romans. Now Titus employed a "secret weapon" — he had Josephus, his most eminent captive, address the Jewish defenders and with every conceivable argument convince them to surrender but, of course, to no avail.

By now, the situation in the city was desperate. Famine and disease were rife, and defections reached 500 per day, sometimes more. Those that were caught by the Romans as they left the city were tortured and then crucified in full view of the city's inhabitants.

Stones toppled during the Roman siege cover a Herodian street near the Western Wall

Winter passed in the besieged city, and during the month of March, the Roman embankments rose towards the Antonia. But John of Giscala and his troops sneaked out to undermine the wood and earthen ramps, daubing them with pitch and setting them on fire that seemed to the Romans to appear out of thin air.

Titus eventually took the Antonia, but could not breach the Temple. Hand-to-hand combat cost many Roman lives. Frustrated and consumed with fury, Titus ordered the construction of a siege wall around

"Judea Capta",
Coin minted after the 70 CE
Roman victory over the Jews

the entire city, fighting every inch of the way. Famine gnawed at the hopeless city; bodies filled every house and alleyway. Titus gave orders to demolish the Antonia and construct a broad ramp against the northwest corner of the Temple where it met the Antonia, and into the Temple courts itself.

Battering rams were brought in a failed attempt to break down the western Temple doors. Titus then gave orders to set the gates on fire. Their silver coverings melted away, and the doors began to burn. Roman soldiers poured in through the charred remains of the doors, but the fire burned itself out.

In fact, Josephus says the Temple burned down against the wishes of Titus. After the Romans had penetrated the inner Temple courts, they were set upon by the defenders. During the fray, fires broke out that were impossible to quench. As the Romans were running the Jews out of the Temple courts, one Roman soldier snatched a burning brand and, lifted up by another soldier, threw it in a window. The fire raged down a passageway around the north side of the inner sanctum, and flames soon engulfed the complex.

What Titus thought when he realized the blaze was burning out of control, no one can know. But one thing was certain: he clearly understood that the Temple was the bastion of the Jewish faith, and as long as it stood victory would elude him.

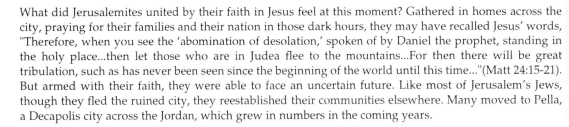

As the flames engulfed the sanctuary and its courts, the enormous limestone blocks of the Temple walls exploded as the stones burst from their places and fell to the pavement 150 feet below. Josephus immortalized the terrible scene: "While the holy house was on fire...ten thousand of those that were caught were slain; children and old men, and profane persons and priests...and as well those that made supplication for their lives as those that defended themselves by fighting. The flame was also carried a long way, and made an echo, together with the groans of those that were slain; and because this hill was high, and the walls at the temple were very great, one would have thought the whole city had been on fire. Nor can one imagine anything either greater or more terrible than this noise. And now the Romans, judging that it was in vain to spare what was round about the holy house, burnt all those places..."(Wars 6: 5:1).

Marble relief depicting the golden
Menorah and other cult
implements of the Temple, carried
by Roman soldiers in a triumphal
parade commemorating Titus'
victory over Jerusalem.
The Arch of Titus, Rome.

What did Jerusalemites united by their faith in Jesus feel at this moment? Gathered in homes across the city, praying for their families and their nation in those dark hours, they may have recalled Jesus' words, "Therefore, when you see the 'abomination of desolation,' spoken of by Daniel the prophet, standing in the holy place...then let those who are in Judea flee to the mountains...For then there will be great tribulation, such as has never been seen since the beginning of the world until this time..."(Matt 24:15-21). But armed with their faith, they were able to face an uncertain future. Like most of Jerusalem's Jews, though they fled the ruined city, they reestablished their communities elsewhere. Many moved to Pella, a Decapolis city across the Jordan, which grew in numbers in the coming years.

Sixty-five years later another blow fell when in the wake of the doomed Bar Kochba Revolt, the remnant of Jews in Judea was exiled to Galilee and beyond. In those days even the name of Jerusalem was changed to a pagan one, Aelia Capitolina, honoring Emperor Hadrian and Jupiter.

The Western Wall, the last
remnant of Herod's Temple

Pagan temples went up, many on Jewish or Christian holy places, in an attempt to obliterate the link of these faiths with their sacred sites. It may have seemed to some that pagans would rule forever. Yet two centuries later — the mere blink of a historical eye — the pagan way of life was gone forever from the Holy Land as the Roman Empire itself became Christian. Ironically, the huge pagan remains, instead of wiping out the memory of the locations of holy sites, actually helped preserve them. Faith in the one God had triumphed. In many of the towns where Jesus had once taught and performed miracles, synagogues and churches went up side by side, burying the pagan shrines beneath them. Over the centuries to come, Judaism and Christianity evolved along their own paths, yet they continued to be both nurtured and bound together by the common roots of heritage and history.

The Many Faces of the Land of Israel

Acre

Mount Hermon

Jezreel Valley

The River Jordan

Caesarea

Samaria

Judea

The Elah Valley

The Dead Sea - Lot's Wife

Nahal Zin

The Antonia Fortress, from the Model of Jerusalem at the Holyland Hotel.

The Temple, from the Model of Jerusalem at the Holyland Hotel.

Solomon's Portico and the Court of the Gentiles from the Model of Jerusalem at the Holyland Hotel.

The hill of Golgotha, from the Model of Jerusalem at the Holyland Hotel.

The Citadel (David's Tower)

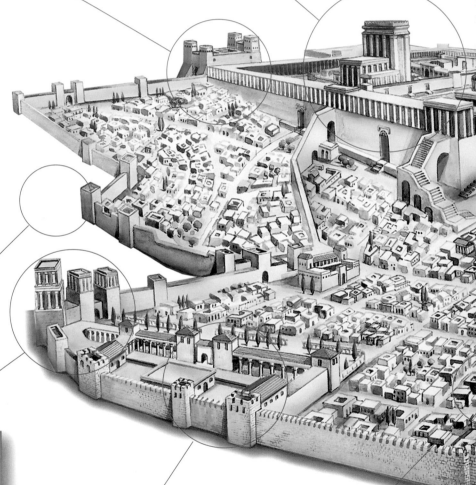

Herod's Palace, from the Model of Jerusalem at the Holyland Hotel.

An affluent home in the Upper City of Jerusalem.

Remains of the grand southern staircase leading to the Temple courts

Vestiges of channels in the City of David, quarried to deliver water to fields in the Kidron Valley.

The Pool of Siloam.

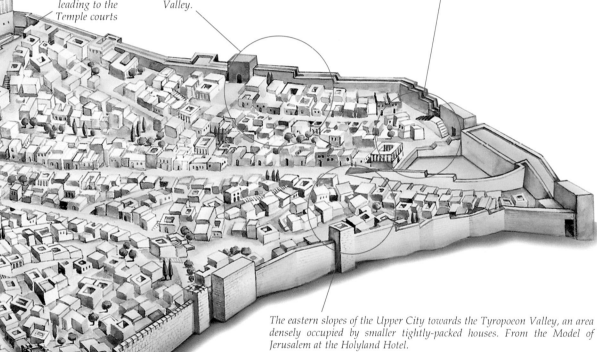

The eastern slopes of the Upper City towards the Tyropocon Valley, an area densely occupied by smaller tightly-packed houses. From the Model of Jerusalem at the Holyland Hotel.

Jerusalem in the time of Jesus

Jerusalem

"Ten measures of beauty were given to the world. Nine were taken by Jerusalem..."
Babylonian Talmud, Kiddushin, 54a

"Wilson's Arch", a Herodian structure near the Western Wall

Before the period of Herod the Great, the Jewish inhabitants of the land mainly eschewed life in the cities. The gentile city, the polis, with its gymnasium, amphitheater and bathhouses, was a cultural anathema to them. It was only when Augustus awarded Herod large tracts of land that previously existing cities came under his aegis. Herod then embellished the cities of Caesarea and Sebastea, and set about beautifying Jerusalem in the Roman style.

During the time of Herod, Jerusalem's population doubled to reach about 60,000 people. The Temple was expanded so that it comprised some one-sixth of the area of the city. A hippodrome was constructed as well as a theater, royal palace and two fortresses (the Antonia and another fortress guarding the palace).

The city's old water supply from the Gihon Spring could no longer satisfy the town's burgeoning population. Dozens of reservoirs were dug in addition to an aqueduct bringing water from pools near Hebron. To avoid the use of bridges, the waterway spanned the 15-mile distance — as the crow flies — by curving round the hills to reach a total length of some 40 miles. It reached various large pools located throughout the city, and one branch, first built in the days of the Hasmoneans, went over a bridge to the northwestern side of the Temple. Wilson's Arch is a remnant of the numerous arches that supported that bridge.

Beautiful homes for the city's wealthy class were built to the south and north of the city. These wealthy people carved out space for themselves in death as well as in life — numerous magnificent tombs attest to the continued expansion of the old necropolis surrounding the city.

Coin of Hasmonean King Alexander Janaeus (103-76 BCE)

The Hasmonean Dynasty

The Hasmoneans were descended from Mattathias, a member of a priestly family descended from Jehoiarib (I Chron. 24:7). Mattathias hailed from Modi'in in Judea and lived during the period of Selucid Greek rule over the land. His opposition to the Selucids' attempt to force Jews to worship the Greek gods led, in 176 BCE, to a revolt spearheaded by his son Judah, known as the Maccabee. During the revolt, the Temple was finally liberated from the Greeks, purified of its idol worship and rededicated to the worship of the one God. This event is commemorated in the festival of Hanukkah.

After independence from the Selucid Greeks, the Hasmonean family ruled the land under the leadership of Judah's brother Jonathan. Jonathan united in himself and in his descendants the functions of high priest, king and military leader. After the death of Jonathan, leadership passed to his brother Simeon and then to his son, John Hyrcanus. Hyrcanus was the great-great-grandfather of Marianne, the famous Hasmonean princess who married Herod the Great.

Originally, the Hasmonean dynasty was supported by the Pharisees, but the Pharisees, put off by the accumulation of wealth and the hellenized ways that characterized the Hasmoneans and their courtiers, criticized the Hasmoneans, and the royal family began actively to persecute them.

The Hasmoneans' possession of both the monarchy and high priesthood was also a source of friction between them and the Essenes, many of whom considered only priests of the house of Zadok (a son of Aaron) legitimate.

The Temple

"the Temple...adorned with beautiful stones and donations..."
(Luke 21:5)

The Offering of Sacrifices

The Hebrew word for sacrifice, korban, comes from the words "come close". Giving up a prize possession on the altar was seen as a prime means of coming closer to God. Among the many laws governing the sacrifices were those stating that the offering had to be the property of the person making it (Lev 1:2); only domesticated animals raised for food were allowed, and the sacrificed animal had to be without blemish.

Animals were slaughtered in the area to the north of the Court of the Israelites (only birds were actually slaughtered on the altar itself). The priest whose turn it was to slaughter the daily sacrifice would begin after sunrise when he heard the great gate leading to the sanctuary being opened. The sacrificial portions were placed on the lower part of the ramp leading up to the altar, together with the flour for the meal offering and the cake offering of the high priest and the wine libation. The priests would cast lots for the privilege of bringing the portions up to the altar itself.

Pilgrims would await the daily opening of the Nicanor Gates to the court in front of the Temple, known as the Court of Israel. From the Court of Israel they could observe the priests slaughtering the sacrificial animal at the moment of the opening of the sanctuary door, and transferring it to the altar in front of the sanctuary. The priests who had been chosen to burn incense on the golden altar inside the sanctuary could be seen entering to perform this enviable task. The heavenly fragrance of the incense wafting from within was legendary.

The blood of the sacrifice was sprinkled on the horns of the altar when the priests had completed their allotted tasks, which included the recitation of blessings and the Ten Commandments, the collecting of the ash from the inner altar, the trimming of the wicks of the candelabrum and the placing of the incense in the sanctuary after glowing coals had been brought by another priest from the outer to the inner altar. On holidays, pilgrims could also see the sacred Temple implements on display, among them the incense pan, the table of the shewbread, and of course the seven-branched candelabrum, which became one of the most enduring symbols in Jewish art.

Details from a 17th century map of the Wanderings of the Children of Israel by J.F. Bernard

The Candelabrum

The Incense Altar

The Table of the Shewbread

Looking towards the Holy of Holies from the Women's Court - Model of Jerusalem at the Holyland Hotel

Upon completion of their tasks, the priests would stand on the steps of the porch. Raising their hands above their heads, they would intone the Aaronic blessing: "The Lord bless you and keep you; the Lord make His face shine upon you, and be gracious to you; the Lord lift up His countenance upon you, and give you peace" (Numbers 6:24-26). Only the high priest did not raise his hands in order not to place them above the crown he wore on which the sacred four-letter name of God was written. After

Many details of the Temple service are known to modern scholars. The memory of the grandeur of the Temple and its appointments was preserved throughout the millennia in the great works of Jewish literature and art.

his benediction, the sacrificial portions were lifted up to the top of the altar and thrown into the fire.

n addition to priests and Levites on duty by roster, ordinary citizens could also watch the sacrifice as representatives of the people of Israel. Though women did not ordinarily proceed beyond the Court of Women, at least one ancient source (the commentary on the Mishnah known as the Tosefta, *Arachim* 2:1) notes that a woman entered the Court of Israelites to be present during the sacrifice which she had personally brought. The "Court of Women" probably got its name from its galleries, from which women observed the dancing during the Feast of Tabernacles.

When the sacrificial service had ended, most pilgrims made an additional stop in a room where donations to the Temple were left. In addition to the famous "half-shekel" tax (Matt 17:24) required of all Jews, donations could be made towards the purchase of frankincense, firewood and other commodities necessary for Temple worship. It was probably opposite this chamber that Jesus called the attention of his disciples to the poor widow who could only afford two small coins (Mark 12:41, Luke 21:1).

The Levite Choir

The Levite Choir accompanied the daily sacrificial service with song. An unusual sound was the signal for them to assemble: the clattering of the rake dropped to the floor at the conclusion of the cleaning of the altar.

There were about a dozen singers, playing some nine lyres and two harps. The choir conductor held the cymbals and two trumpeters stood on either side of him. The children of the singers stood at the foot of the dais.

The Levite repertoire consisted mainly of Psalms specifically chosen for the particular day of the week or holiday. The public sometimes sang with the choir, such as Psalm 118, when the congregation gathered in the courtyard chanting responsively "his mercy endures forever".

The Levites also accompanied special services with song and music, such as the festival of the drawing of the water on the Feast of Tabernacles when they stood on the steps leading to the gates of Nicanor to accompany the dancers.

Ritual Immersion

"For the Pharisees and all the Jews do not eat unless they wash their hands in a special way, holding the tradition of the elders." (Mark 7:3)

Ritual immersion bath discovered on Masada.

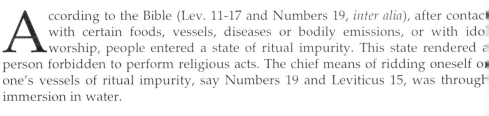

According to the Bible (Lev. 11-17 and Numbers 19, *inter alia*), after contact with certain foods, vessels, diseases or bodily emissions, or with idol worship, people entered a state of ritual impurity. This state rendered a person forbidden to perform religious acts. The chief means of ridding oneself of one's vessels of ritual impurity, say Numbers 19 and Leviticus 15, was through immersion in water.

During the time of Jesus, people were particularly preoccupied with issues of ritual cleanliness. Mark 7:3-4 reflects this preoccupation. "When they [the Pharisees] come from the marketplace, they do not eat unless they wash. And there are many other things which they have received and hold, like the washing of cups, pitchers, copper vessels, and couches." Defilement by contact with the dead was also a concern. In Matthew 23:27 Jesus refers to "dead men's bones and all uncleanliness".

A ritual immersion pool, known in Hebrew as a *mikveh*, must contain at least 40 seah—some 85 gallons—of water. At least some of the water had to be "living water" i.e., rain water, river water or seawater that had not been previously stored in a vessel and was let into the main pool from an adjacent reservoir. "Living water" was a term Jesus knew well and used in his encounter with the Samaritan woman when he engaged her on the subject of water (John 4).

Although later Jewish law would mandate the exact dimensions of the ritual bath there were many variations in dimensions of baths discovered from the time o

Jesus. Some were so shallow that immersion must have been accomplished lying down. Some scholars believe that small pools adjacent to the main pools were used for purifying vessels or for the washing of hands by those who were strictest in their ritual practices.

Numerous ritual baths were discovered in Jerusalem near the southern steps to the Temple Mount. Some of these baths, as well as a ritual bath found at Qumran, have a division in the steps, apparently a kind of "before and after" passage. A reference to this practice may be contained in a third century fragment of an apocryphal gospel known as the Oxrhynchus Papyri (V 840). In the passage, Jesus is accused of not immersing before visiting the Temple and answers: "I am clean, for I have bathed myself in the pool of David. I have gone down by the one stair and come out of it by the other, and I have put on white garments that are ritually clean, and in that state I have come here and looked upon these holy vessels."

Second Temple-era ritual immersion bath near the Temple Mount

This ritual immersion bath is patterned after those discovered in excavations. The round object at the top of the steps may have been for cleaning feet before stepping into the pool. Some baths had smaller basins like the one depicted here, perhaps for the ritual cleansing of vessels, as noted in Mark 7:4.

Sanhedrin members, with the High Priest at center, await the arrival of their colleagues to begin a session.

This chamber, built of meticulously carved ashlars, was discovered near the underground portion of the Western Wall. The Sanhedrin's meeting place in the Temple courts, "The Chamber of Hewn Stone", may have resembled it.

The Sanhedrin

The Sanhedrin was a council of sages that formed the highest political, religious and judicial authority of the Jewish people in the Roman period. The Sanhedrin, whose name comes from the Greek word meaning "council", was made up of 71 members. As Acts 23:6 notes, at the time of Paul's appearance before the body the Sanhedrin was composed of two factions, the Pharisees and the Sadducees. How the two parties functioned together within the council is unclear. One opinion says that each party dominated the council in turn. Others believe that there were three "small sanhedrins" of 23 judges each, who met jointly in order to deliver judgment on matters of weighty national importance, and were headed by a team of two leaders. This opinion suggests that it might have been a Sadducee-dominated Sanhedrin that interrogated Jesus (Acts 4:1-3, Acts 5:17-18-21).

But after 135 CE and the failure of the second revolt of the Jews against the Romans brought about the exile of Jews from Jerusalem and Judea, the Sanhedrin moved to the Galilee where, with time, its powers declined and eventually it was de-legitimized by the Romans.

The Sanhedrin met daily in the Temple in the Chamber of Hewn Stone, adjacent to the court of the Priests. Apparently its deliberations were open to the public, for an early commentary on Deuteronomy 14:23 says: "When one brings the sacrifices that one has vowed to the Temple, he enters the Chamber of Hewn Stone and sees the sages and their disciples sitting and engaging in the study of Torah. The sight inspires him also to study Torah."

"As soon as it was day, the elders of the people, both chief priests and scribes, came together and led him into their council..."

(Luke 22:66)

The High Priest

The Pharisees and the Sadducees

The meaning of the word "Pharisee" is uncertain. It may come from the Hebrew word parash, meaning separate. The name may have been applied to the group by the Hasmonean king John Hyrcanus, who opposed them in favor of the aristocratic Sadducees and expelled them from the Sanhedrin. The Pharisees themselves applied a different meaning to the word, deriving from the Hebrew word "interpret".

The Pharisees were the interpreters of the Torah. They taught that everything is pre-ordained but that people have the free will to choose their path. They believed in the resurrection of the dead, one of the principle doctrines that divided them from the Sadducees, and one that made their sect attractive to the masses, who lived under great duress and difficulty in their daily lives. Pharasaic belief in the coming of the Messiah was one they had in common with the Essenes. On the other hand, their creed that all of history is pre-ordained made them averse to the philosophy of the Zealots, who taught that the Romans could be removed by violent intervention. The Pharisees, while loyal to the teachings of the Torah and significantly involved in matters of ritual purity, were also distinctly humanitarian and practical in their interpretation of it.

Both the Pharisees and the Sadducees acknowledged the importance of the written law, the Torah. But the Pharisees also believed in the possibility of interpretation of the Torah, which became known as the Oral Law. The Sadducees, on the other hand, would not accept anything unless they could trace it directly back to the written law.

The Sadducees were aristocrats, people of means. Their harsh religious rulings and rejection of belief in an afterlife made them appear severe. Josephus says they were gruff and distant from each other in conversation, even if they were acquainted. Among the Sadducees was the family of Annas, who sent Jesus bound to Caiaphas (John 18:24) and who imprisoned the Apostles (Acts 5:17).

Jesus was severely critical of both the Pharisees and the Sadducees. On the other hand, many of Jesus' actions demonstrated his connection to Pharasaic customs, such as the donation of the half-shekel to the Temple. His teaching methods were also those employed by the Pharisees. And he exhorted his followers to listen to the Pharisees that sit in Moses' seat (Matt. 23:1), although not to behave as they did because "they say, and do not do" (Matt. 23:3).

Many Pharisaic themes in the teachings of Jesus, such as the kingdom of heaven and repentance as well as emphasis on belief in the coming of the Messiah, the End of Days, miracles and angels, made Pharisaic Judaism fertile soil for early Christianity to flourish. Paul was a Pharisee (Acts 23:6, Acts 26:5), a pupil of one of the most eminent pharisaic figures of the period, Rabbi Gamliel, who in Acts 5:34 is shown defending the early Christians. So were Joseph of Arimathea, Nicodemus, and some early members of the church (Acts 15:5).

Pharisaic emphasis on teaching in the synagogues led to their exerting a major influence on Judaism in the wake of the destruction of the Temple and becoming the most widespread of Jewish philosophical sects.

Pilgrimage

"Now about the middle of the feast Jesus went up into the temple and taught. And the Jews marveled, saying, 'How does this man know letters, having never studied?'"

(John 7:14-15).

"Whoever has not seen Herod's building has never seen a beautiful building in his life. Of what was it constructed? Of marble stones in variegated colors, blue, red and green. Herod wanted to overlay the stones with gold, but the sages told him 'leave it be'. This way it is more beautiful, for the stones have the appearance of the ocean's waves. " (Babylonian Talmud, *Baba Batra* 4a)

"...you shall seek the place where the Lord your God chooses, out of all your tribes, to put His name for His dwelling place; and there you shall go. There you shall take your burnt offerings, your sacrifices, your tithes, the heave offerings of your hand, your vowed offerings, your freewill offerings, and the firstborn of your herds and flocks. And ...you shall rejoice in all to which you have put your hand, you and your households, in which the Lord your God has blessed you." (Deut 12:5-7)

From the days of Solomon, Jews from all over the world came to the Temple in Jerusalem at least three times a year, on Passover, the Feast of Tabernacles and Pentecost as mandated in Exodus 23:14.

At holiday time, the city of Jerusalem would burst at the seams with tens of thousands of pilgrims. Many would spend their nights in Bethphage, Bethany or other nearby villages. Others would seek shelter in private homes. Pilgrims also stayed in tent cities, which went up in the valleys surrounding Jerusalem. Most pilgrims arrived in the city with beasts of burden carrying all the food needed by the family during their stay, as well as animals intended for sacrifice. Pilgrimage was a joyous occasion and as Jerusalem came into view, pilgrims would break into song and dance.

Many pilgrims made their way to the Temple even before dawn. After bathing in a ritual bath, either in the home in which they stayed or in one of the many baths that surrounded the Temple Mount, they would stream in through the Temple's many gates. A special custom pertained to those who entered by the double gates in the southern wall known as the Huldah Gates. Normally, to ensure orderly traffic, the crowd would enter from the right gate, and when departing, exit from the left. But if one was in mourning, one did the opposite, entering from the left and exiting from the right. In this way, when a fellow pilgrim met a person coming at him or her in the gate, even if the two hailed from opposite ends of the world and shared no common language, a blessing and word of comfort could be offered. Levite guards stood at all Temple gates to prevent the entrance of lepers and reminding all that ritual ablutions must be accomplished before entering the Temple.

In addition to observing and taking part in the majestic Temple ceremonies, people came to the Temple to hear the teachings of their sages and rabbis. John 10:22-24 described just such a scene, with Jesus teaching in the Temple precinct during the festival of Hanukkah.

Opposite page:
Pilgrims gather near the junction of the western and southern walls of the Temple. A portion of the Huldah gates is seen at right, and Robinson's Arch at left.

Fragment of Greek inscription forbidding the entrance of gentiles to the inner Temple courts

A portion of the southern Huldah gates (believed to be the Gate Beautiful of Acts 3:2) towers above visitors

"Robinson's Arch" supported steps to the Temple in Jesus' day

The Antonia Fortress

A troop of soldiers

"Then the soldiers of the governor took Jesus into the Praetorium and gathered the whole garrison around him."

(Matt 27:27)

Herod built the Antonia Fortress, named for his patron Mark Antony, shortly after he captured Jerusalem in 37 BCE, on the site where the Baris, the Hasmonean stronghold, once stood. The Antonia was located in one of the most strategic spots in the city. Atop a 150 foot high rock escarpment, it was designed to protect the northern section of the city which lacked natural defenses. The Antonia also commanded a sweeping view of the Temple courts in order to allow Herod's soldiers to spot and stop a brewing insurrection.

Rock escarpment on which the Antonia Fortress once stood

It was precisely this situation that the Roman garrison (probably consisting of a cohort — 480 men) faced when Paul was seized by the crowd. When the incident was reported to the Roman commander, "He immediately took soldiers and centurions and ran down to them. And when they saw the commander and the soldiers, they stopped beating Paul. Then the commander came near and took him, and commanded him to be bound with two chains; and he asked who he was and what he had done. And some among the multitude cried one thing and some another. So when he could not ascertain the truth because of the tumult, he commanded him to be taken into the barracks. When he reached the stairs, he had to be carried by the soldiers because of the violence of the mob...Paul said, 'I am a Jew from Tarsus, in Cilicia, a citizen of no mean city; and I implore you, permit me to speak to the people'. So when he had given him permission, Paul stood on the stairs and motioned with his hand to the people. And when there was a great silence, he spoke to them in the Hebrew language, saying, 'Brethren and fathers, hear my defense before you now'" (Acts 21:30-22:1).

The Antonia, whose interior measured 360 x135 feet, was no spartan military barracks. In addition to its military components, it contained luxury apartments and baths. Reported Josephus: "by its magnificence, it seemed a palace" (Wars of the Jews 5:5:8).

A centurion

The Centurion.

Commander of the century, the centurion was the backbone of the Roman army's lower echelon of command. To his soldiers, he was a cross between a company commander and a sergeant major. Centurions were sometimes appointed as district officers and had various responsibilities towards the local population. The centurion was often an educated man from a wealthy family, which would enable him to make the "contributions" to his superiors necessary to help him climb the ladder of success.

Two centurions are mentioned in the New Testament. Cornelius, stationed in Caesarea, was the first pagan to become Christian. The centurion in Capernaum, whose servant Jesus healed, was probably on hand to guard the Roman tax monies moving through the town. He used his wealth, according to Luke 7:5, to build the town synagogue.

Opposite: The Antonia Fortress. At far right is Paul preaching to the crowd from the steps, as mentioned in Acts 21:40.

The Struthion Pool, dug into the moat of the Antonia Fortress by Herod

The Roman Army

Inscription of the Tenth Roman Legion Fretensis

Enlistment in the Roman Army most often took place between the ages of 18-23. Among the most important requirements of a recruit was height — at six Roman feet, he towered over the local population. Once selected, a four-month course of basic training would begin, but not before the soldier was tattooed and given a seal bearing his name, which he would wear around his neck for the duration of his service.

Though service was long (some twenty-five years!) and soldiers were forbidden to marry, its benefits were great. A regular salary was awarded (according to some scholars about 50 dinars per year) and expenses defrayed. Although wealth was an advantage for a recruit, even the poorest recruit could accrue recognition, and eventually wealth, by distinguishing himself in the service of the Emperor.

A Roman legion, numbering between seven to ten cohorts (3500-6000 men), had been stationed near Jerusalem since 35 BCE, sent in by Antony to quell another of the seemingly endless uprisings by the Hasmoneans, this time by Antigonus' sister. Herod supported the legion himself because although the Romans may have been willing to support Herod in his bid to disperse his enemies, they would not consider useful a client king whose reign needed constant shoring up with Rome's forces. Herod's force was put together in the tried and true Roman style, based on the operative unit of the cohort, which itself was composed of six centuries of eighty men each. In addition to cavalry, infantry and artillery branches, Herod's forces included a navy, based at his new city of Caesarea, and an intelligence branch.

The battering ram:
A beam, 60-100 feet long, was suspended from a horizontal beam and put into motion by means of ropes fastened to the beams. To protect the soldiers operating the beam, a sort of house was built over them. A ram's head was affixed to the beam.

Many of the troops in Herod's standing army were foreign mercenaries, which included Thracians, Germans, Gauls and a unit he enlisted from the region of Mount Lebanon, Sebastea and elsewhere. Many other members of Herod's army were of his own Idumean ethnic background. He often settled these troops in villages where they would live an ordinary village life, farming plots of land awarded them, but maintaining patrol and battle readiness.

The ballista:
Operated like a crossbow by two soldiers, it had an effective range of 500 yards. It was sometimes mounted for defense on fortress towers.

But most of Herod's soldiers were Jewish, joining him during the time he was consolidating his rule after receiving the crown from the Romans. "Many came in to him", reports Josephus, "some induced by their friendships with his father, some by the reputation he had already gained himself, and some, in order to repay the benefits they had already received from them both. But still, what engaged the greatest number on his side was the hopes from him, when he should be established in his kingdom..."(Wars of the Jews 1:15:4) Three times the size of a typical Roman garrison, Herod's army was indeed a formidable force.

Roman troops were a common sight in every town and city.

34

Crucifixion

"And when they had come to the place called Calvary, there they crucified him, and the criminals, one on the right hand and the other on the left." (Luke 23:33)

The execution of Jesus by crucifixion has forever focused the attention of the world on this cruel mode of capital punishment. In 1968 in Jerusalem, the first-ever discovery was made of the bones of a crucified man, shedding new light on the manner of the death of Jesus. Among the skeletal remains was the right heel bone of a crucified man. Embedded within was an 11.5 cm long iron nail, with wood fragments beneath the nail head which have been identified as olive wood. The position of the nail within the bone indicates that the man was crucified with his feet on either side of the upright of the cross. The hands and arm bones of the skeleton were found undamaged. It is therefore probable that the upper limbs were tied, rather than nailed, to the cross.

An archaeological find giving unique historical evidence about death by crucifixion in the time of Jesus. The heel bone (the calcenaeum—the largest bone in the foot) of a crucified man pierced with an iron nail.

Death by crucifixion (probably the "hanging on a tree" mentioned in Deuteronomy 21:23) was so cruel that hanging by the neck may have been introduced later as a more humane form of execution. One Jewish source notes that a crucified person might be "redeemed" — by bribing the Roman guards — even at a point very close to death, by a wealthy passerby. This would indicate that the crucified person could remain alive for a long time. Medications were sometimes administered to ease pain, such as the soporific myrrh (Mark 15:23).

As the hours progressed, and the crucified person became weaker, the body would collapse against the cross, the feet coming into contact with a protrusion of wood placed beneath them. The cause of death was often asphyxiation, as the weight of the body hanging in such a manner prevented the muscles that controlled breathing from proper functioning. As another act of mercy, the legs would be broken (John 19:31) so that the feet could not rest on the "shelf". Breathing would then be further impeded, hastening death.

The place of Jesus' crucifixion was called "the Place of the Skull" perhaps because of the shape of the rock at the execution site. The shape of a skull (calvarium in Latin) can clearly be seen in this photo of Gordon's Calvary at the Garden Tomb, in Jerusalem.

Wood was scarce in Jerusalem. It is therefore possible that rather than carry the entire cross to the place of crucifixion, Jesus may have carried only the crossbar with the upright kept permanently at the site of execution and reused. A naturally growing tree could also have been used for this purpose. The trees in this photo can be seen at the Biblical Resources Scripture Garden in Ein Karem.

Crucifixion, with all its cruelty, was meant to be viewed by passers-by who could see and be warned of Rome's wrath. Thus the site of crucifixion was often outside the city gates (Hebrews 13:11) and along main roads.

A Wealthy Household in Jerusalem

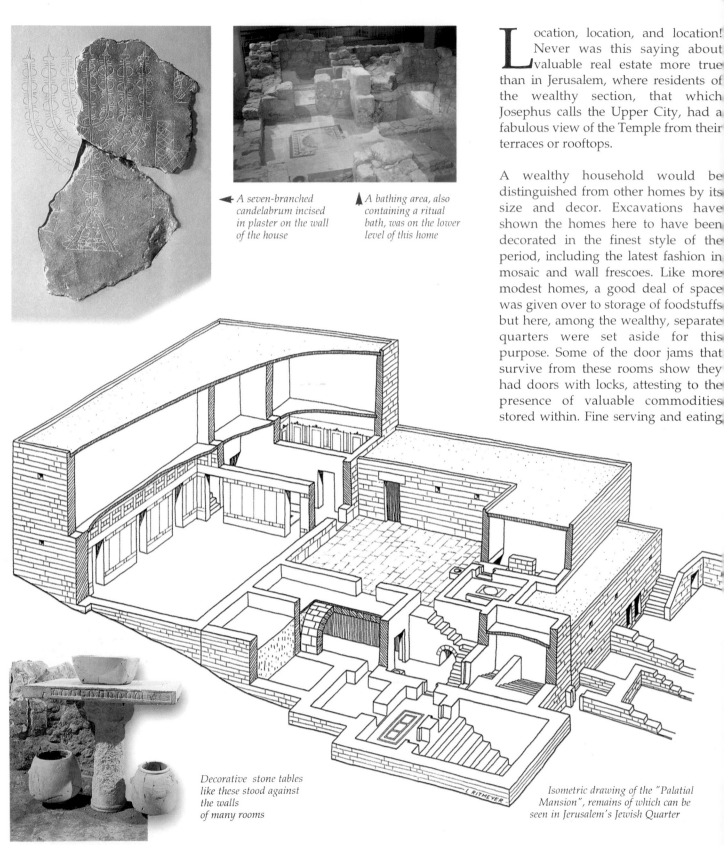

A seven-branched candelabrum incised in plaster on the wall of the house

A bathing area, also containing a ritual bath, was on the lower level of this home

Location, location, and location! Never was this saying about valuable real estate more true than in Jerusalem, where residents of the wealthy section, that which Josephus calls the Upper City, had a fabulous view of the Temple from their terraces or rooftops.

A wealthy household would be distinguished from other homes by its size and decor. Excavations have shown the homes here to have been decorated in the finest style of the period, including the latest fashion in mosaic and wall frescoes. Like more modest homes, a good deal of space was given over to storage of foodstuffs but here, among the wealthy, separate quarters were set aside for this purpose. Some of the door jams that survive from these rooms show they had doors with locks, attesting to the presence of valuable commodities stored within. Fine serving and eating

Decorative stone tables like these stood against the walls of many rooms

Isometric drawing of the "Palatial Mansion", remains of which can be seen in Jerusalem's Jewish Quarter

utensils, especially glass and elegant clay tableware adorned with floral motifs, were a part of every wealthy household.

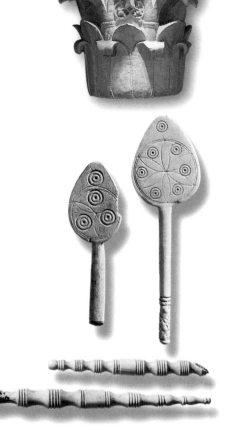

This particular home had its own ritual bath. This could not be considered a luxury in a period when many considered ritual cleanliness of paramount importance, especially in this part of town where many priests lived. A particular concern revolved around the ritual purity of objects and vessels used in daily life. By Second Temple times, the preferred material for such vessels was stone, which was considered not susceptible to ritual impurity, and many stone vessels were discovered in excavations in Jerusalem. Water was often stored in stone jars to keep it from ritual impurity and so have it at the ready for washing before meals, as John 2:6 relates: "Now there were set there six waterpots of stone, according to the manner of purification of the Jews, containing twenty or thirty gallons a piece."

Like most wealthy homes throughout the empire, this home had few or no windows facing the street. The life of the household went on in an enclosed courtyard. Beneath the courtyard was a water cistern, essential in a city rainless for eight months of the year.

Numerous stone implements attest to a well-developed stoneware industry in Jerusalem of the first century.

This room, discovered in the central block of the mansions, may have been the main living room of one home.

A typical village from the time of Jesus

The Village

*"Then Jesus went about
all the cities and villages,
teaching in their synagogues,
preaching the gospel
of the kingdom..."
(Matt. 9:35)*

Reconstructed village scene

Villages always sought well-protected locations, especially before the Pax Romana (which came with the ascension of Augustus to power in 27 CE) provided a sense of security to the countryside. People shied away from open areas in the plains, choosing slopes with a good view of the road and a not-too-distant water source.

According to Josephus (Life, 45:235), there were 240 villages scattered throughout Galilee. The average area of a village might be no more than a few acres, with a population of a few hundred souls. Larger villages, called "towns" by Josephus, might comprise some ten acres, and were often walled. In one such community, Nain, Jesus meets a funeral procession at the gate and raises a widow's son from the dead (Luke 7:11).

On the outskirts of the village was the market, where inhabitants could purchase the few commodities they did not manufacture themselves. Just beyond it were workshops of the tanner and the potter, situated where the smells created during manufacture would waft away on the prevailing eastern wind.

"Now as soon as they had come out of the synagogue, they entered the house of Simon and Andrew, with James and John," reads Mark 1:29. Let us imagine Jesus and the disciples walking through streets like those depicted in the drawing on the previous page. They would have walked along unpaved alleyways, often no wider than the width of a camel laden on either side with bales of flax. Courtyards closed in by plastered stone walls, some ten feet high on either side, gave privacy to their inhabitants. No-one standing at a window could have announced the arrival of Jesus, for these windows were situated high in the walls and were quite small, designed only to admit light and air. As the group progressed, they may have greeted the occasional shopkeeper, perhaps a vendor of knives or rope or a butcher, whose doorways, unlike those of the homes, faced the street.

*Precariously perched on a promontory
surrounded on all sides by steep ravines,
the location of the town of Gamla
is an example of its inhabitants' search
for a protected site.*

A hand mill for grinding grain

Villagers of the Holy Land in Jesus' day, like agrarian societies today, used and re-used their tools, even when broken or impaired, as demonstrated by the following commentary regarding the laws of ritual purity as they applied to implements used in daily life: "...The size of what remains of them must be in every case such that they can do their wanted work...If a shovel has lost its blade it still remains susceptible [to ritual impurity]...because it is become like a hammer..." (Mishnah, Kelim 12:2-3)

Numerous containers of various sizes and shapes were part of every household's possessions.

A plough

Implements used in everyday village life have changed little over thousands of years.

A comb-rake

A shovel

This iron-studded sledge was used for threshing. Sometimes a child sat astride it to give it added weight.

A broom-rake

A Village House

"...they entered the house of Simon and Andrew, with James and John".   *(Mark 1:29)*

We can imagine that the house of Peter's mother-in-law in Capernaum looked much like the house in the drawing at right. Arriving at the house, Jesus and the disciples would pass through the courtyard, encountering members of the household busy at their daily tasks, weaving, caring for the farm animals, grinding corn or baking bread. Perhaps they dodged children at play as they stepped over the high threshold. Pulling aside the curtain hanging over the door, they entered the house. Pausing momentarily while their eyes adjusted to the dimness within, they then made for the bedroom in which they could see, by the flickering light of a small oil lamp, the form of Peter's mother-in-law lying motionless on a pallet.

"So he came and took her by the hand and lifted her up, and immediately the fever left her. And she served them. Now at evening, when the sun had set, they brought to him all who were sick and those who were demon-possessed. And the whole city was gathered together at the door."   *(Mark 1:31-33)*

Model of houses in Capernaum from Jesus' day

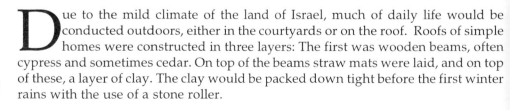

Restored ovens from ancient Katzrin

Life on the Rooftop

"In that day, he who is on the housetop, and his goods are in the house, let him not come down to take them away. And likewise the one who is in the field, let him not turn back." (Luke 17:31)

Due to the mild climate of the land of Israel, much of daily life would be conducted outdoors, either in the courtyards or on the roof. Roofs of simple homes were constructed in three layers: The first was wooden beams, often cypress and sometimes cedar. On top of the beams straw mats were laid, and on top of these, a layer of clay. The clay would be packed down tight before the first winter rains with the use of a stone roller.

This type of roof would have to be "broken through" (Mark 2:4) by chopping a hole, as in the following story: "And when they could not come near him because of the crowd, they uncovered the roof where he was. So when they had broken through, they let down the bed on which the paralytic was lying." Luke's version of the same story (Luke 5:19) has the man let down "through the tiling". In the village setting, tiled roofs were less common. Luke is believed to have been a native of Antioch in Syria, and his choice of words probably reflects his city background.

Working in the Fields

"The kingdom of heaven is like a man who sowed good seed in his field; but while men slept, his enemy came and sowed tares among the wheat and went his way. But when the grain had sprouted and produced a crop, then the tares also appeared." So the servants of the owner came and said to him, 'Sir, did you not sow good seed in your field? How then does it have tares? He said to them, 'An enemy has done this.' The servants said to him, 'Do you want us then to go and gather them up?' But he said, 'No, lest while you gather up the tares you also uproot the wheat with them. Let both grow together until the harvest, and at the time of harvest I will say to the reapers, 'First gather together the tares and bind them in bundles to burn them, but gather the wheat into my barn.'" (Matt 13:24-30)

The harvest

Separating the wheat from the chaff

Ploughing

Each day except the Sabbath, during the early morning hours, farmers might walk some two hours to reach their vineyards, wheat and barley fields, and olive groves, which covered some twelve acres per family. Especially during periods of intense cultivation, many farmers would have built lean-tos in the field and lived in these from Sunday morning to Friday, the eve of Sabbath. Some villagers might work land owned by others who lived in the larger, walled towns of the Galilee, Tiberias or Sepphoris for example.

"A certain man had a fig tree planted in his vineyard, and he came seeking fruit on it and found none. Then he said to the keeper of his vineyard, 'Look, for three years I have come seeking fruit on this fig tree and find none. Cut it down; why does it use up the ground?' But he answered and said to him, 'Sir, let it alone this year also, until I dig around it and fertilize it. And if it bears fruit, well. But if not, after that you can cut it down.' " (Luke 13:6-9)

A vineyard in Cyprus, from which some of the best wine of the time of Jesus was imported.

Domestic Animals

Which of you shall have an ass or an ox fallen into a pit, and will not straightaway pull him out on the Sabbath day?" (Luke 14:5)

Domesticated animals were the backbone of rural life. In the absence of carriages and carts, which had difficulty navigating the rough country roads and village streets, the mule or donkey was all-important as a pack animal. While sheep and goats were kept in pens on the outskirts of the village, the mule, the ox and the cow were kept in a stable adjacent to the courtyard of their owner and accessed through the courtyard, where chickens ran freely.

Goat's milk, a staple of life

As described in Proverbs 27:26-27 "...lambs will provide your clothing, and the goats the price of a field; You shall have enough goats' milk for your food, for the food of your household, and the nourishment of your maidservants' animals." Animals were slaughtered for food only on festive occasions, at which time their skin could be prepared for use as clothing, water-carriers and butter-churns. Goat and sheepskin could be prepared for use in the writing of sacred scrolls. Pigeons were raised for food on the outskirts of the village in columbaria, or dovecotes. Pigeons and domestic animals were also raised to be brought by the family to Jerusalem for sacrifice in the Temple.

At the well

Horses were expensive to buy and keep, and therefore were owned mostly by aristocrats. In the city, horses were also ridden by guards on patrol. A horse too old to ride long distances was used to push the grinding wheel of an olive press or grain mill.

The sages appreciated the uses and beauty of domesticated animals, as seen in the following quote from tractate *Brachot* of the Jerusalem Talmud: "When you see a beautiful camel, a beautiful horse, or a beautiful donkey, say 'blessed is He who creates beautiful things in His world'."

The camel was a common beast of burden, used by traders.

The Shepherd

"What man of you, having a hundred sheep, if he loses one of them, does not leave the ninety and nine in the wilderness, and go after that which is lost, until he find it?". (Luke 15:4)

Because of their frequent appearance in the Bible, as well as their importance to the daily lives of the people, sheep and their shepherd often appear symbolically in New Testament writings.

At first when Jesus related the now-famous shepherd's parable in John 10:1-5, the audience did not grasp his point (John 10:6). However, he continued in the same vein, amplifying the image by adding numerous minutiae of a shepherd's daily life (John 10: 7-18).

At the time of Jesus, in the days before the destruction of the Second Temple, farmers and herders often lived in harmony. In the Galilee, most non-arable areas were set aside for herding. These areas were called *midbar* and are sometimes mistakenly translated as "desert", but they come from the Hebrew word meaning the place "to lead the flocks" and were often a valuable part of a farmer's holdings. The younger people in the family would herd the sheep and goats while the seniors would supervise cultivation on other tracts.

Not everyone saw shepherds in a positive light, especially after the destruction of the Temple. As Torah study became an increasingly prominent feature of Jewish life, the fact that many shepherds practiced their craft in outlying areas far from the centers of learning became a reason to disparage them. Rivalry between shepherds and scholars is reflected in the words of the famed second century scholar Rabbi Akiva, who in his early years was unlettered and worked as a shepherd for his wealthy future father-in-law. He admits that in those days, "Had I had a scholar in my hands, I would maul him like an ass" (Babylonian Talmud, *Pesachim* 49b).

Such harsh words had their roots in the disastrous economic changes that were visited on many Jews in those days. Many farmers had lost land or were trying to rehabilitate holdings decimated by war, a task made difficult by the sheep and goats which encroached upon them, and shepherds found themselves cast out by other members of society.

"The good shepherd"

A Roman-era sheep enclosure.

Sheep grazing near Bethlehem

The Olive Press

The olive press in this drawing is patterned after one discovered at Gamla from the first century CE. It was of the "beam and weight" type, less common in the Galilee where this stage of oil production was accomplished with pressure exerted by a screw on a column of straw baskets.

In preparation for the pressing, the olives were heated to express the oil more readily from the fruit, an operation carried out in the grove-owner's home. The olives went through three pressings: the first stage produced the best oil, a second and third pressing continued the process of expression, which was completed over a twenty-four hour period.

In the first stage of production, the olives were crushed by a round crushing mill. The crushed olives were then inserted into round baskets stacked on the round press-bed. A wooden beam inserted into a recess in the wall hung over the press-bed. The "fulcrum" of the beam was the column of baskets. On the beam were hung weights of 600 pounds each, that could be lowered into niches in the floor.

The oil was often sold next door to the press. Some presses belonged to individuals, others to a cooperative. When the press was individually owned, payment for pressing was in a percentage of oil, plus the residue from the crushed olives which was used as fuel.

Adjacent to the olive press at Gamla, a ritual bath was discovered. The Mishnah notes that olive oil, like wine, was to be produced in a state of ritual purity. For this reason, Diaspora Jews preferred oil produced in the Holy Land, counting on observance of this precept here and doubtless providing the economic base for dozens of villages throughout the country at this time.

"And if some of the branches were broken off, and you, being a wild olive tree, were grafted in among them, and with them became a partaker of the root and fatness of the olive tree, do not boast against the branches."
(Romans 11:17-18)

Restored ancient olive press at Beit Guvrin, which used stone weights to exert pressure.

An oil press discovered at Capernaum. This type of press used a screw to exert pressure, and was more advanced than those that used stone weights.

The Blacksmith

"His feet were like fine brass, as if refined in a furnace..."   *(Rev. 1:15)*

A modern blacksmith using ancient techniques

The ancient "village smithy" performed an important service for his neighbors.

The blacksmith's trade was an important one in Jesus' day, as metal was used in every aspect of life, from weapons to household items to jewelry and coins.

The highest ranking metal workers were apparently those who produced jewelry and other ornaments. The ordinary metal worker was called a *nappah,* coming from the Hebrew word "to blow", referring to the bellows used to keep the fire hot enough to soften the metal. For fuel, the smith used charcoal which he produced himself. A reference in the talmudic tractate *Shabbat* notes that it is permitted on the Sabbath to burn coal to forge a knife for a circumcision that is to occur that day. Iron was mined in Jordan, but the Talmud records that the best iron for making weapons came from India.

The process of producing iron tools provided the rabbinic sages with several analogies, among them, "he who bathes in hot water without showering himself afterwards with cold water is like iron that has been treated in fire without being put in cold water afterwards" (Babylonian Talmud, *Shabbat,* 44a).

The Carpenter

A restored wooden threshing sledge of the type used in ancient times

"Is this not the carpenter, the Son of Mary, and brother of James, Joses, Judas, and Simon?"
(Mark 6:3)

Modern commentators note that the Greek word for Jesus' profession was *tekton*, and could refer to any of several building trades. Workers in wood, however, were common in Jesus' day, carrying out some of the more professional aspects of construction which the householders themselves could not perform. In fact, besides the architect, or master-builder (1 Cor 3:10) the carpenter may have been the only paid worker on a building site. A carpenter, says an ancient commentary on Exodus, can be recognized as a professional by his possession of a toolkit containing the tools of the trade. Among the carpenter's jobs were the doors and shutters for the windows of the house.

A sawhorse similar to the kind used in ancient times

Reconstructed wooden stage from the theater at Sepphoris, a town near Nazareth that Jesus may have known .

In addition to doors and shutters, carpenters installed locks (seen on the table) and crafted agricultural tools as well as those parts of furniture made of wood.

The Weaver

"Now the tunic was without seam, woven from the top in one piece." (John 19:23)

There are many references in ancient Jewish texts to the preparation of cloth, from the sowing of the flaxseed, the combing of flax, to spinning and weaving. That spinning was done outdoors is understood from a talmudic reference to gossips "who spin their yarn by moonlight" (*Sotah* 6a) and the "sinner, [who] spins in the street" (*Ketuboth* 7b). Linen was sometimes imported from Egypt, although local production was also known, with linen coming mainly from Galilee and wool from Judea.

The most common loom mentioned is a standing loom with the warp stretched between an upper and a lower beam, or with loom weights stretching the warp. A treadle loom is mentioned in the Talmud (*Shabbat* 105a) as being worked by men.

All of the family's clothes and blankets were woven in the home, using a standing loom, with weaving begun at the top of the garment.

The upright loom was the most common in Second Temple times. This reconstructed loom is hung with clay loom weights found at Masada .

A fragment of cloth, among many discovered at Masada

Clothing

"And from him who takes away your cloak, do not withhold your tunic either." (Luke 6:29)

Various forms of dress had great symbolism in the Roman world. A toga of natural, undyed wool was a sign of citizenship. A toga with a purple band was worn by a magistrate, while a dark wool toga indicated mourning and whitened wool, a politician. Among farmers, a short tunic was the norm for work.

Two pieces of clothing were usually worn by both men and women: a poncho-style undergarment, and a mantle draped over it, usually removed when indoors. The undergarment was sometimes made of linen, although numerous references to "linen and purple" (Luke 16:19, Revelation 18:16 *inter alia*) show that pure linen garments were a rich person's prerogative. Women also wore a headdress when they went out in public. Jewish males of the time of Jesus did not always wear a head covering.

The mantle was made of one piece of cloth (John 19:23). To the mantle, the ritual fringes required by the Bible (Numbers 15:37-41 and Deut 22:12) were fixed. Ancient commentaries tell us that the length of these fringes was not standard at the time of Jesus, as does Jesus' criticism of the Pharisees who "enlarge the borders on their garments" (Matt 23:5) to show piety. The mantle could be worn in a number of ways—thrown over the back of the neck and fastened with a brooch or over one shoulder.

The most costly form of purple dye was manufactured from the secretion of the murex trunculus *sea-snail. Purple signified royalty; the Roman expression parallel to the modern "blue-blood" was "purple-blood". Recent research shows that this pure purple dye, Tyrean Purple (biblical* argaman*) when exposed to sunlight becomes the sky-blue tekhelet, one thread of which was required as part of the ritual fringes. Lydia (Acts 16:14) was a dealer in purple, and therefore likely to have been a wealthy and influential woman. For those who could not afford the real thing, imitation purple was derived from the hyacinth flower and other sources.*

The Grain Mill

"...give us this day our daily bread..."   (Luke 11:3)

Putting one's nose to the grinding stone was more than just an expression at the time of Jesus. Grinding of wheat and corn was done daily, just enough to bake that day's bread, giving new significance to the famous words from the Lord's Prayer. About ten pounds of flour could be produced in one hour's grinding on the large two-part hourglass-shaped grinder. Grinders were often constructed of basalt, a hard rock that would stand up to the wear-and-tear. The conical lower half of the mill was topped by a pivoting hourglass-shaped stone. Grain was poured into the top, ran down through a small opening between the top and bottom stone and then into a trough, often incised into the base of the lower stone. A donkey's entire life could be spent turning the grinding stone, but unhappy was the horse that thus may have finished an illustrious career, when too old or weak for other tasks.

Smaller, round grinding stones were meant to be operated by hand while seated, and could produce about two pounds of flour per hour.

The grinding of each day's grain into flour was the task of the women of the household.

Games

Children played quoits or ball games. Games of dice were played by adults, with pieces made of glass, ivory or metal. One popular game was played on a game-board divided into twenty-four parts by twelve parallel lines and one transverse line. Ball games were played, sometimes in teams, with balls filled with air or stuffed with feathers. A kind of volleyball was played where a ball was thrown up into the air and players standing nearby tried to catch it.

"Game boards" were often carved into a street's paving stones, such as this one in Sepphoris in the Galilee. Designs etched on the late Roman-era paving stones known as the Lithostrotos, beneath Jerusalem's Sisters of Zion Convent, are believed to have been used in a dice game called, "the Game of the King".

Ancient dice made of stone.

A Typical Synagogue of Jesus' Day

The size and appointments of the synagogue depended on the means of the villagers or townspeople it served, who took it upon themselves to build and maintain this most important of community institutions.

The Synagogue

"And when he had come to his own country, he taught them in their synagogue..."
(Matt 13:54)

True to the Greek translation of its name, the synagogue at the time of Jesus was first and foremost a place of assembly. The few first-century synagogues so far unearthed by archaeologists are simple structures with almost none of the elements that would characterise them in later times, such as mosaic floors or inscriptions. Still, they were usually the largest building in the village, and with their clerestories or gabled, tiled roofs, stood out from the flat clay roofs surrounding them.

Though prayer in the synagogues was not unknown (Matthew 6:5), the main religious activity that took place in the synagogue was the reading of a Torah portion on the Sabbath and holidays, its translation into Aramaic or Greek, and a reading from the Prophets, as Luke describes (Luke 4:16-17). As a sign of respect for the Holy Scriptures, Jesus would probably have stood to read the Torah, possibly on a wooden dais in the center of the room. But unlike modern-day teachers and preachers who stand to deliver their message, in order to address the congregation, he would have taken the seat reserved for the teacher known as the "Moses seat" (Matt. 23:2).

In the days of Jesus, a particular order of reading the Torah or the Prophets had not yet come into being, so Jesus may have chosen the passage himself on that Sabbath day in Nazareth. The discussion which Luke records in the wake of Jesus' reading from Isaiah (Luke 4:16-28) would have been typical of the synagogue atmosphere in those days before prayer was a regular and central part of synagogue routine. Not silent reverence, but dialogue and discussion, and probably a great deal of milling around before or after the readings and teachings (or even during them) took place.

People could seat themselves on the stone or wooden benches that lined the synagogue walls, or on mats on the floor. Such a day it must have been when, in "one of the synagogues", Jesus healed a crippled woman on the Sabbath day (Luke 13:11-17). The event was denounced by the synagogue ruler, but in the end Jesus seems to have won that particular, very public, debate.

This vignette also highlights the presence of women in the synagogue without reference to any kind of separation based on gender. Speaking in Thessalonica over three Sabbaths to a congregation that also included women, Paul converted many of them (Acts 17:4). Early writings note that women could be called to read from the Torah as long as a man had read first, and only in the later writings of the Babylonian Talmud women were barred from reading the Torah in public.

Jewish sources trace the idea of the synagogue to the early days after the destruction of the First Temple and the words of Ezekiel 11:16 "Therefore say, Thus says the Lord God: Although I have cast them far off among the gentiles, and although I have scattered among the countries, yet I shall be a little sanctuary for them in the countries where they have gone."

This interpretation allowed the synagogue — the "little sanctuary" — to evolve from a place of gathering, adding elements both liturgical and architectural that would eventually allow the synagogue to evolve into the house of prayer that it is today.

The Thanksgiving Scroll from Qumran, similar in appearance to Bible scrolls read in synagogue in the days of Jesus

The synagogue at Masada, used in the first century by the Sicarii inhabitants of the palace-fortress.

Remains of the first century synagogue at Gamla in the Golan Heights.

Education

Schooling was among the most binding obligations of a father to his son and originally the father was his child's teacher. Later, according to the Jerusalem Talmud, schools were established by King Alexander Janaeus (in the first century BCE), to educate fatherless boys. The purpose of education was not to impart social status or a trade (the teaching of a trade being the task of the father) but rather to teach the Torah with an eye to inculcating correct moral behavior.

Children learned to read Torah beginning at five years of age. At ten, they began the study of the Oral Law, commentaries of the sages on various biblical passages. Because these were the days before the invention of vowels in Hebrew, students had to listen intently to their teachers to catch the correct pronunciation of every word.

School was often held in the main room of the synagogue, with wooden benches that could be removed when class was not in session. Classes began early in the morning, continued until a break in the afternoon, and then resumed in the evening. Studies were conducted every day of the week, including the Sabbath eve and Sabbath itself. The maximum number of students in a class was ideally twenty-five, above which the teacher was entitled to an assistant.

Girls did not usually attend school, although it is assumed that because their future role in educating their own children was great, they did receive an education at home at the hands of their father or mother.

Ideally, the teacher, like other public servants, was not to take money for his services. In a commentary on Deut 4:5 "surely I have taught you statutes and judgments", the *Nedarim* tractate of the Jerusalem Talmud states: "what I have given freely you must give freely". But payment to teachers is mentioned in many cases. Parents would pay the teachers individually, and tuition for poor children was covered by public funds.

An inkpot

"Having then gifts differing according to the grace that is given to us, let us use them...he who teaches, in teaching..." (Romans 12:6-7)

Shard inscribed with the alphabet, perhaps a scribal exercise

Writing implements like those pictured here (wax tablets that could be reused) were rare. Much ancient education depended on listening to the teacher. Significantly, Jesus repeats the words "You have heard it said" (Matt 5:21) several times in his teachings in the Sermon on the Mount.

The Babylonian Talmud (Gittin 36a) tells of one teacher who lost his position because he used to beat his students, but who was later reinstated after no substitute could be found to replicate his impeccable pronunciation!

A Wedding Feast

"He who has the bride is the bridegroom; but the friend of the bridegroom, who stands and hears him, rejoices greatly because of the bridegroom's voice. Therefore this joy of mine is fulfilled."　　　　　　　　　　　　　　　　　　　　　　　　　　　　*(John 3:29)*

The engagement ceremony was the first essential step in marriage. During the festivities accompanying the engagement, which took place at the house of the bride's father, a contract would be written and signed by the groom and witnesses, outlining the economic and social obligations of the future husband to the bride. The groom would then seal the contract by giving the bride an item of value, which could be very modest.

If the future bride was very young (engagements took place as young as 12 years of age), she could defer the move into the groom's home and the beginning of married life for several years. In any case, she was given at least 12 months to prepare her clothes and jewelry. The husband used this period to prepare the home as well as the festivities of the marriage itself.

The wedding took place in the evening, when the bride was brought to the groom's house in a festive torchlight procession. A hint of this custom can be found in the words of Jesus: "the kingdom of heaven be likened unto ten virgins, which took their lamps, and went forth to meet the bridegroom" (Matthew 25:1).

Beforehand, both bride and groom bathed and were anointed with aromatic oils and dressed in their finest clothes, saved especially for the occasion. The guests, too, wore their best attire — in fact, it was considered an insult to come improperly dressed (Matt. 22:11-12). Revelation 21:2 uses the phrase "prepared as a bride adorned for her husband" as a way to describe the unimaginable beauty of Jerusalem at the end of days.

When the family and all the neighbors were gathered in the house or courtyard, a gala meal would begin. But before the meal, the guests would ritually purify themselves by washing their hands. This custom is reflected in John 2:6: "Nearby stood six stone water jars, the kind used by the Jews for ceremonial washing." We know that at the meal the wine flowed freely (John 2:2-3). During the meal, poetry would be read and songs sung, and gifts presented to the couple.

Monetary remuneration was part and parcel of every betrothal negotiation.

Divorce

Jesus' own views about divorce are set out in Mark 10:11-12: "...Whoever divorces his wife and marries another commits adultery against her. And if a woman divorces her husband and marries another, she commits adultery." The Mishnaic tractate called Gittin ("bills of divorce") sets out the conditions for termination of a marriage. One view was that of the strict school of Oral Law that existed at Jesus' time, the School of Shammai, which said "a man may not divorce his wife unless he has found unchastity in her" (Mishnah, Gittin 9:10). On the other hand, the more liberal School of Hillel, in a purposefully exaggerated expression designed to challenge the strict view, says: 'even if she spoilt a dish for him' (Gittin 9:10).

Ancient Delicacies and Daily Bread

"Now when he had brought them into his house, he set food before them; and he rejoiced, having believed in God with all his household." (Acts 16:34)

Among simple folk, people sat on the floor or on mats to take their meals, helping themselves to food placed in the center. But in a wealthy household, or at a festive meal, the guests reclined on a three-sided divan, and the food would be brought by servants from side rooms. The host was seated second from the left facing the open side of the table, with places of honor (Luke 14:7) reserved on either side of him (Matthew 20:21).

At a simple meal, people used their pliable wide flat bread as both spoon and plate, scooping out food from the common large dishes. Bread would be dipped in vinegar as a spice. Leftover pieces of this bread, perhaps the "crumbs which fell from the rich man's table" of Luke 16:21, are thought to have served as a kind of napkin for wiping the fingers. Even in the remains of average homes in town or country, however, archaeologists have discovered quite a wide range of vessels, both for serving and for eating.

One source tells of the weekly supply of food that a husband was required to supply his wife, a landlord his laborers, and the community to the poor: about 4.4 liters of wheat, 1 1/4 liters of lentils, 1/4 liter oil and about 2.2 liters of dried figs or other fruit. Oranges and lemons were exotic; the groom might bring one to his bride. Sweets included honeycomb (Luke 24:42).

For festivals and the Sabbath day, it was customary to offer as fine a menu as one could afford. "Killing the fatted calf" (Luke 15:27) was a sign that a festive meal was in preparation. Meat was consumed only on the Sabbath or festivals and only rich people ate meat every Sabbath. The sages saw the purchase of special foodstuffs for holidays as a way of further "advertising" the celebration. When asked what food would differentiate the Sabbath from the weekday meal, one rabbi answered: "a pie of fish hash and flour".

Wine was a common beverage. It was used in a ritual context for celebrating the Sabbath, festivals and to enhance other joyous occasions, as well as for medicinal purposes. Often it was diluted with water, a practice which some experts have suggested helped disinfect the water from the diseases it was prone to in antiquity. Good local wine came from Samaria, the best imported was from Cyprus and Rhodes. Another popular drink was made from date juice and from lotus jujube.

A Menu and Recipe for a Typical Festive Meal

Salad: Mint, rue, coriander, parsley, chives, green onion, lettuce, coleroot, thyme, carmint, green fleabane, celery.
Main Course: Roast lamb with hot mint sauce.
Side dishes: Chard made into salad with lentils and beans, mustard as a green vegetable, artichoke.
Dessert: Pear compote made with dried pears boiled in wine and water together with honey. Pomegranates could be served off season (i.e., not in the summer or fall) because they had been placed in hot sea water until discolored, and dried 3 days in the sun, then re-hydrated by placing in cold fresh water overnight.
Dried apples mixed with toasted sesame.

Ancient stone anchors
from the Sea of Galilee

Fishermen

"And Jesus said unto them, Come ye after me, and I will make you to become fishers of men."
(Mark 1:17).

Jesus' first disciples were fishermen, and so these words must have resonated deeply within them. There are many links between their daily work and the new task Jesus brought them. A skilled fisherman had to know that for different types of fish, different nets needed to be used. He understood that lack of teamwork could lose him his catch, and lack of patience could leave his nets empty. Choice of the right fishing grounds and sensitivity to nuances of wind, depth and temperature had to be second nature to him in order to bring in the catch.

Fishing is the backdrop for many a Gospel story, and knowledge of the kind of nets used by Jesus' first fishermen-disciples brings new understanding to these stories.

There were three types of nets in use in the days of Jesus: the seine (dragnet), the cast net and the trammel net, usually made out of linen thread. Each type of net is mentioned in the Gospels in relation to a different kind of fishing:

THE DRAGNET

The dragnet was operated by two teams. One team took the net, which was like a wall some 100 feet long and 12 feet high and attached by ropes at each end. The bottom side of the net was weighted by sinkers. First, the boat made for the best fishing-ground. In the Sea of Galilee, the warm springs of Tabgha on the north shore must have been a favorite of the disciples. One team alighted, holding one side of the net with thick ropes. The boat sailed out with the rest of the crew until the net was stretched and then circled back to shore at a distance that allowed the net to become fully spread. Then the other team took out the other rope. Both teams harnessed themselves to each end of the net and dragged it to shore.

The dragnet was the longest and heaviest net used by Sea of Galilee fishermen and required a larger boat to maneuver it into place. The famed ancient "Galilee Boat", may have been the type of boat used for this kind of work.

THE CAST NET

When Jesus encountered Simon and Andrew, they were probably using the cast net, a circular net about 20 feet in diameter with weights attached to the bottom edge. The cast net could be thrown either from a boat or from the shoreline. With great skill, the fisherman folded the net over one arm in a manner that would allow

A contemporary net

Ancient net
weights

t to open completely when it landed in the water and then descend like a parachute, trapping fish beneath it. To retrieve the cast net, the fisherman would dive into the water and pull the bottom of the net together carefully.

Because the cast fisherman was required to jump into the water frequently to retrieve his net, his usual garb was...nothing! In the story of the miraculous catch of fish in John 21, when Peter heard that Jesus was standing on the shore, "he put on his outer garment (for he had removed it), and plunged into the sea" (John 21:7). Let us not imagine Peter dressing himself fully before jumping into the water! Rather, he had probably just been preparing to dive into the water to retrieve his cast net when he heard that his teacher was waiting. Too anxious to wait until the boat reached the shore, he jumped into the water and swam the distance. Before jumping in, Peter put on the minimal amount of clothing necessary to appear respectfully before Jesus.

Artist's rendering of the "Galilee boat"

THE TRAMMEL NET

The trammel net was actually three nets in one: two large mesh walls about five feet high, in between which was sandwiched a net of finer mesh. The net would be piled into the boat and one end would be slipped into the sea. It would then be slowly pulled around by the boat until a circle, a kind of open ended barrel, was created. The fish caught within would attempt to escape by pushing themselves against the larger, inner net. They would find themselves entrapped in the finer mesh and as they attempted to swim on, catch themselves in the larger mesh net. Jumping fish, like the St. Peter's Fish (tilapia), could be caught by attaching a collar-like net on a reed frame around the top of the "barrel". Each evening before the night's fishing began, and after every throw of the net, the fishermen extricated each fish from within the mesh, cleaning and mending the nets as did James and John, the sons of Zebedee (Matthew 4:21).

THE ANCIENT GALILEE BOAT

In 1986, the outline of a wooden boat was discovered mired in the mud on the northwestern shore of the Sea of Galilee. By its shell-first, mortise-and-tenon method of construction, pottery vessels discovered with it, and the carbon-14 test, the boat could be conclusively dated to the first century CE. Its dating to one of the most important periods in the history of the Holy Land makes the vessel of unparalleled significance to both Christians and Jews . The 24 by 7 foot-long craft, made of seven different species of wood including cypress and cedar, seems to have been continuously repaired over many years by a master craftsman, but in the end was apparently abandoned on the shoreline. Its burial for two thousand years in a muddy, anaerobic environment allowed for the extraordinary state of its preservation. After years of work to replace the water that clogged its wooden fibers with a wax-based substance, the boat is now on display in a special exhibition hall at Kibbutz Ginossar, not far from the site where it was first discovered.

*Drawings and text based with permission
on the research and publications
of Mendel Nun, Kibbutz Ein Gev.*

The Dragnet

*"Again, the kingdom of heaven is like a
dragnet that was cast into the sea and
gathered some of every kind, which, when it
was full, they drew to shore; and they sat
down and gathered the good into vessels, but
threw the bad away."*

(Matt 13:47-48)

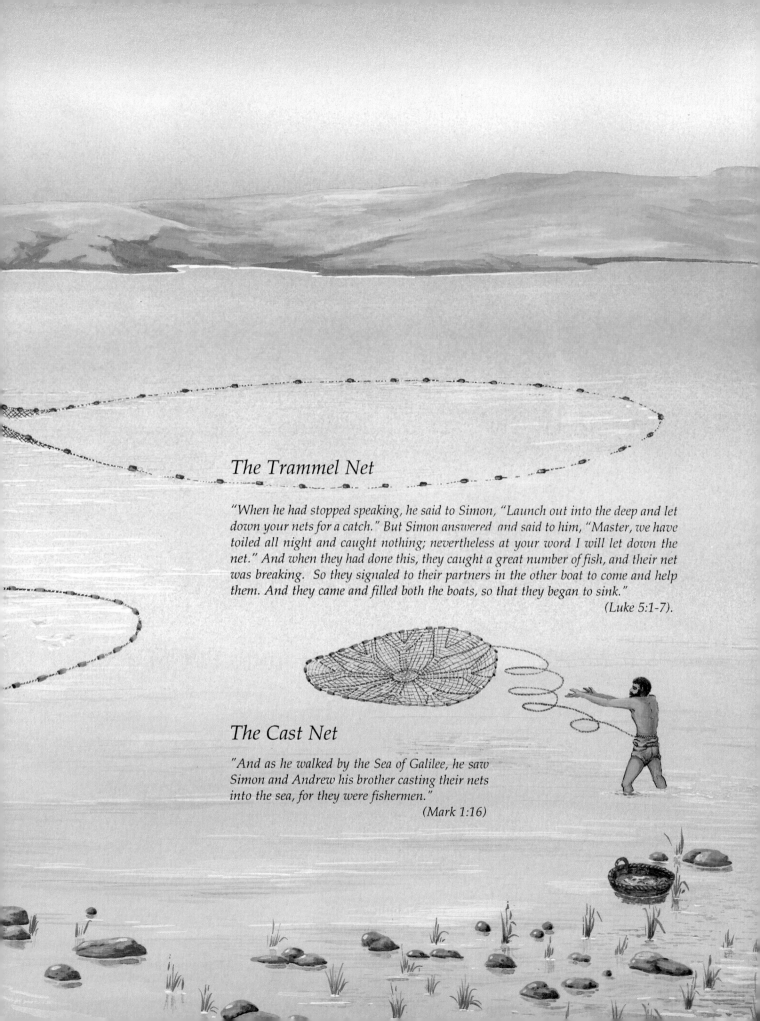

The Trammel Net

"When he had stopped speaking, he said to Simon, "Launch out into the deep and let down your nets for a catch." But Simon answered and said to him, "Master, we have toiled all night and caught nothing; nevertheless at your word I will let down the net." And when they had done this, they caught a great number of fish, and their net was breaking. So they signaled to their partners in the other boat to come and help them. And they came and filled both the boats, so that they began to sink."

(Luke 5:1-7).

The Cast Net

"And as he walked by the Sea of Galilee, he saw Simon and Andrew his brother casting their nets into the sea, for they were fishermen."

(Mark 1:16)

A Countryside Manor House

"It is like a man going to a far country, who left his house and gave authority to his servants, and to each his work, and commanded the doorkeeper to watch."　　　　　*(Mark 13:34).*

Josephus describes a wealthy country home as "a large castle, and no way unlike a citadel" (Life 48:246). Archaeological evidence has begun to bear out his words, showing that all such farms thus far excavated share four elements: an olive press, grape press, a tomb and a protective tower some 33 feet high and containing several rooms. Some also had ritual baths. Such a home often had an interior courtyard, enclosed by other dwellings belonging to the same extended family.

Such manor farms began when people purchased land more than two and one-half miles walk (the limit of a convenient daily journey) from their village of residence, eventually moving from the village to a house on their land. On such a holding olives, grapes, wheat or barley would be grown. Of course, the wealthier the farmer, the larger his holdings. "Who is rich?", says the Babylonian Talmud *(Shabbat, 25b).* "He who owns one hundred vineyards and one hundred fields, and one hundred slaves to work them."

The homes of the larger farms could be termed "manor farms" or rustic villas. These homes contained both living quarters and an industrial area containing a wine or olive press. On the upper floor of the two-story villa were the living quarters of the lord and his family. The lower floor housed various foodstuffs and other supplies. In the parable of the man going to a far country (Mark 13:34), the doorkeeper acted as the manor house "security guard". He would be on duty both to keep the house safe from marauders, as well as to be ready at a moment's notice to announce the master's arrival so the other servants could be roused to their duties.

Some 50-70 people could occupy such a complex on a permanent basis. Most of these homes were built of field stones or roughly dressed stones, but carved column drums and capitals have also been unearthed in some excavations, attesting to the owners' attention to aesthetic details in the construction and design of their country homes.

Sources of the period relate that tenant-farmers were subject to an onerous taxation burden: they paid one-third of their harvest to the landowner (and another third to the king). Jesus' parable of the landowner whose tenant-farmers greeted his rent collectors with violence (Matthew 21:33-41), must have rung familiar to the audience.

Close to 70% of the arable land in the northern part of the country was cultivated at the time of Jesus, owned by landed gentry. The landowner, with his servants, crops, managers and accountants, must have been a well-known figure to residents of the Galilee, precisely the reason why Jesus based so many parables on this character.

The owner of the property, as Matthew points out, did not usually reside permanently on the premises (Matt:21:33). However, his manager did live on the property. Such a manager is mentioned in Jesus' parable about "a certain rich man who had a steward..." (Luke 16:1)

Drawing of imaginary manor house based on excavations in the Carmel region.

The Ways of the Wealthy

Cosmetics dishes and applicators

A comb with teeth small enough to remove lice, a common affliction

Necklace, rings and robe-fasteners discovered at Masada

Pins for fastening outer tunics

" ...a woman came having an alabaster flask of very costly oil of spikenard. " (Mark 14:3)

As in our own day, in ancient times it was the wealthy class that had both leisure time and the means to pamper themselves. Roman ladies took care of their complexion with nightly facial masks. One mask, made of dough and ass's milk, was said to have been invented by Nero's wife Empress Popaea. So much ass's milk was required by Nero's wife, Pliny records, that an entire herd of she-asses accompanied her wherever she went!

Face powder was either white or red and mineral-based, moistened with saliva or mixed with an oil base. Veins at the temples were outlined with blue, brows and lashes were painted black or brown. Kohl, another form of blue, was painted over the eyelids and believed to have medicinal properties. Fingers and toenails were often painted white.

Oil was used as a hair dressing, as indicated by Mark 14:3. Women's hair was held in place with beeswax and sometimes piled high atop the head. Some of the hairdos were so intricate that the Talmud *(Shabbat 94b-95a)* forbids undoing a woman's hairdo on the Sabbath because it would mean transgressing the prohibitions of "building" and "demolishing"! Contrary to popular imagination, only wealthy men had long hair, which required special care.

Among the most interesting pieces of jewelry worn by wealthy women in talmudic times was a "Jerusalem of Gold", a crown depicting the walls of the Holy City. In the talmudic tractate *Shabbat* (59a) the sages discussed whether it was proper for a woman to wear this heavy crown on the Sabbath day.

The lady of the manor examines her reflection in a copper mirror, while her husband enjoys the fruits of his vineyard.

A Manor House Wine Press

The treading floor

"There was a certain landowner who planted a vineyard and set a hedge around it, dug a winepress in it and built a tower...".   *(Matt 21:33)*

A common stationary form of winepress was created by quarrying the treading floor from a rocky surface that was scored with channels leading the juice from a higher to a lower point into a shallow reservoir in which the residue would settle. The reservoir was divided into compartments, and the clarified juice drained through an aperture in the divider into the neighboring compartment. From here the juice was collected in clay jars and sealed with a mud cork, leaving a small opening through which carbon dioxide could escape during the fermentation process. Depending on the size of the treading floor, one or more persons would work in the treading of the grapes.

Much rabbinic discussion revolved around wine production by Jews, since wine produced by Gentiles for the purpose of idol worship (known as "libation wine") was strictly forbidden. Jews were to drink wine produced only by other Jews, and that wine was to be produced under conditions of ritual purity. For this reason, archaeologists often find a ritual immersion bath adjacent to a winepress.

The man who owned this winepress probably hired his servants in a manner similar to the wealthy landowner of Jesus' parable (Matt 20:1-13), although that landowner's methods of payment were certainly unorthodox, a fact that would have kept the audience in suspense until the meaning of the parable was revealed.

A Doctor and His Patient

"So he took the blind man by the hand and led him out of the town. And when he had spit on his eyes and put his hands on him, he asked him if he saw anything. And he looked up and said, "I see men like trees, walking." Then he put his hands on his eyes again and made him look up. And he was restored and saw everyone clearly."
(Mark 8:23-25)

Healing in the Days of Jesus

In the ancient world, healing of the sick was often the task of religious leaders. The Pharisees understood that healing could occur through intervention when they referred to the healing of a blind man by Jesus as in the realm of "such miracles" (John 9:15-16).

Demons were often seen as the cause of illness. Casting out of demons, therefore, was a widespread form of healing. In many New Testament instances of demon-possession, the tormentors are noted in the plural, such as "legion" in the story of the Miracle of the Swine (Mark 5:9).

Remains of the Pools of Bethesda

Diseases of the eye, like the one afflicting this man undergoing treatment, were a common affliction in antiquity. Blindness is mentioned numerous times in the New Testament. In the story of the blind man and the pool of Siloam, Jesus applies a salve of earth from the pool and saliva to the eyes. Among the ancient physician's tools was a special long case (seen on the table at right) that held a plant derivative called collyrium, stored in the form of long sticks, which when needed was combined with water to form a paste.

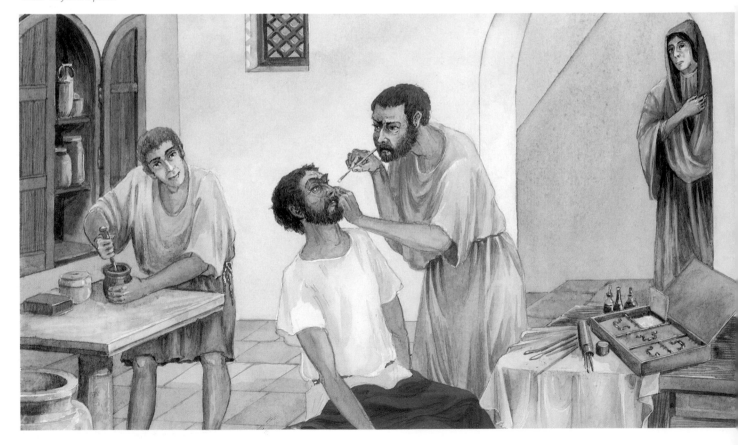

The "high fever" mentioned in the story of Peter's mother-in-law (Luke 4:38-39) was a specific illness that might be identified with chronic malaria. Jesus healed Peter's mother-in-law by touching her hand (Matt 8:15, Luke 8:54). He healed Jairus' daughter in the same manner, as well as a leper (Matt 8:3, Mark 1:41, Luke 5:13). Among the Essenes, whom Josephus tells us studied "whatever is of use to the body and the spirit" (Wars 2:8:6), healing through touch was also known. The Apostles used anointing oil in the healing process, as noted in Mark 6:13 and Luke 10:34. Physicians had special assistants whose task it was to anoint patients with a prescribed oil specific to the illness.

THE POOLS OF BETHESDA

A pagan who was ill usually went to a temple of Asclepius, the pagan god of healing, or to a shrine to the goddess Hygenia. Often he or she would remain there for several days, waiting for a sign or a dream regarding the course of the disease or its treatment. Pagan priests of Asclepius were often physicians, or pretended to be. Archaeologists have noted that a pagan healing shrine to Asclepius was later located at the pool of Bethesda, where Jesus commanded a paralytic to walk. Some note that the story of the angel: "For an angel went down at a certain season into the pool, and troubled the water: whosoever then first after the troubling of the water stepped in was made whole of whatsoever disease he had" (John 5:4) was probably not connected to any known Jewish ritual.

The Talmud mentions over 400 plants which were used as pharmaceuticals. Among them was cumin, now recognized to contain infection-preventative substances, which was applied to wounds.
The gum of the terebinth tree (above) was used for toothaches and halitosis.

The Pools of Bethesda, as seen in the Holyland Model of Second Temple-era Jerusalem.

Hot springs were known in antiquity for their therapeutic effects. In the Mishnah, two therapeutic hot springs are mentioned repeatedly: those of Tiberias on the Sea of Galilee and those of Gadara not far from there. It has been suggested that the many sick people who flocked to Jesus were often those who had come to the famous hot springs of the region in search of a cure.

Another curative indigenous to the Holy Land was asphalt, obtained from the Dead Sea, which was applied to boils and for pest extermination.

Burying the Dead

"When Joseph had taken the body, he wrapped it in a clean linen cloth, and laid it in his new tomb which he had hewn out of the rock; and he rolled a large stone against the door of the tomb, and departed."
(Matt. 27:59-60)

Jewish burial customs required that a body be buried as soon as possible after death, as were Sarah (Genesis 23:2-4) and Rachel (Genesis 35:19). Even an executed criminal, says Deuteronomy 21:22-23, should be buried before nightfall. Caring for human remains is considered one of the highest forms of a good deed as it is carried out without expectation of a favor returned.

Numbers 19:16 declares, however, that anyone who touches a human bone or a grave will be considered ritually unclean. Therefore, elaborate regulations evolved, among them the prohibition in antiquity of burial within the confines of a town. Burial was also not permitted on the Sabbath day. For this reason, after Jesus' death on the cross, Joseph of Arimathea requested that the body be released to them to be buried before the Sabbath began, putting off some burial rituals until the Sabbath was over (Mark 16:1, Luke 23:56).

The so-called Tomb of Absalom, in reality a second-century BCE tomb in Jerusalem's Kedron Valley.

The practice of bringing aromatic spices to the tomb (Luke 23:56) derived from the necessity of disguising the smell of decay for the benefit of those visiting the tomb for mourning rituals in the first days after or for additional burials. For this reason, the tomb was sometimes closed with a rolling stone, as seen in this drawing.

Burial with one's family is an important biblical tradition going back to the days when Jacob's dying wish was "...to be gathered to my people; bury me with my fathers in the cave that is in the field of Ephron the Hittite in the cave that is in the field of Machpelah, which is before Mamre in the land of Canaan, which Abraham bought with the field of Ephron the Hittite as a possession for a burial place" (Genesis 49:29-30). David also, as 1 Kings 2:10 records, "slept with his fathers", a phrase which repeats itself numerous times with reference to the kings of Israel and Judah.

The Tomb of the Sons of Hezir in the Kedron Valley

Any person, whether rich or poor, was entitled to a proper burial. From the moment of death, the body would not be left unattended, and the family of the deceased would be comforted by the presence of numerous friends to see to their needs. The body would be washed, as was Tabitha whom Peter raised from the dead (Acts 9:37).

Burial in caves was a practice carried out by the wealthy who could afford to purchase the land and hew out the shelves and niches in the cave. Poor people were buried in the ground in shaft graves about six feet deep and twenty inches long.

Many would accompany the body to the burial place, as is recorded in the funeral at Nain "...a dead man was being carried out... And a large crowd from the city was with her" (Luke 7:12). Professional mourners might be hired, who would accompany the bier barefoot. The procession might stop several times on the way to the gravesite to recite psalms. During or before the procession, music might be played (Matthew 9:23) and torches held aloft.

The remains of the deceased were anointed with spices and clothed in special wrappings (John 19:39-40). An interesting reference to this practice comes from an anecdote in the ancient commentary *Genesis Rabba*, in connection with the story of the death of Jacob: "When Rabbi Johanan was about to be taken from the world, he said to those who had to attend to him, "bury me in gray clothes which are neither black nor white, so that if I arise and stand among the righteous, I shall not be ashamed, and if I stand among the wicked, I shall not be confounded". When Rabbi Josiah was about to be taken from the world he said:"...bury me in white garments, for I am not ashamed of my deeds, and I am fit to meet the countenance of my Creator". Grave clothes are mentioned in the story of the burial of both Lazarus (John 11:43) and Jesus (Matthew 27:59).

Jerusalem's Second Temple era Tombs of the Kings

Belief in the resurrection, common among the Pharisees, dictated many burial customs, chief among them the custom of secondary burial: in the case of cave burials, about a year after bodies had been laid to rest on a shelf or in a stone sarcophagus or wooden coffin in a cave that served as a family burial place, family members would enter the tomb, collect the bones and place them in a small box known as an ossuary, often inscribing on it the name of the deceased and sometimes a warning against opening the box. Such warnings did not prevent thieves from looting graves in search of valuable personal effects that were sometimes buried with the deceased, and most graves discovered by archaeologists were disturbed by grave robbers in antiquity.

A richly decorated first century ossuary discovered in excavations on the grounds of the Dominus Flevit Church on the Mount of Olives

An ossuary inscribed with the name "Caiphas", likely a descendant of the high priest of the same name (Matt. 26:57, John 18:24)

Seeking Desert Solitude

"In those days John the Baptist came preaching in the wilderness of Judea and saying, 'Repent, for the kingdom of heaven is at hand!'" (Matt 3:1-2)

Seeking out the purity of the desert as a path to spiritual renewal was a well-known phenomenon in Judaism. It was part of a long tradition going back to the days of Moses and Elijah, both of whom sought out the rigors of the desert. John the Baptist preached his message from the wilderness, and Jesus "was led by the Spirit into the wilderness to be tempted by the devil" (Matt 4:1) while fasting for forty days. In time, Christian monks would go to the desert in an effort to emulate this lifestyle and that of Jesus and John the Baptist.

In Second Temple times many Jews, not necessarily sectarians, left home and family for varying periods of time to experience desert solitude, or to seek out a valued leader. Josephus, as a part of his education, spent three years in the wilderness, learning at the feet of a teacher "whose name was Banus...and used no other clothing than grew upon trees, and had no other food than what grew of its own accord, and bathed himself in cold water frequently, both by night and by day, in order to preserve his chastity" (Life of Josephus, 1,11).

In Luke 7:24-25, Jesus makes note of this drift to the wilderness in connection with the ministry of John: "What did you go out into the wilderness to see? A reed shaken by the wind? But what did you go out to see? A man clothed in soft garments? Indeed those who are gorgeously appareled and live in luxury are in kings' courts. But what did you go out to see? A prophet? Yes, I say to you, and more than a prophet."

Caves in Qumran in the Judean desert in which seekers of solitude may have lived

A teacher preaches in his cave-classroom in the desert. His "student body" would have changed weekly or monthly, as some disciples returned to their daily lives with new pupils taking their place at his feet.

Qumran

Clay pots and oil lamps found at Qumran

Scholars had long been aware of the ruins standing atop a marl plateau on the northwestern coast of the Dead Sea. After the 1947 discovery of the Dead Sea Scrolls in caves not far from these ruins, archaeologists turned their attention to them. The first excavation was led by Father Roland De Vaux of the Dominican Ecole Biblique. He viewed the ruins as a monastic center, identifying a scriptorium where the scrolls were written, a dining hall, a meeting room, a hoard of coins and other aspects of a centrally organized community. These details fit the description of the Essene lifestyle in the writings of Philo, Pliny and Josephus. Father de Vaux and others believed that the members of the community lived in caves, or in tents whose wooden poles have been discovered, preserved in the region's dry climate. A large cemetery with very simple tombs is another indication of the austerity of the lifestyle of Qumran's inhabitants.

Over the years, other scholars have tried their hand at alternative theories about Qumran. Some scholars believe that a direct route linked Jerusalem to Qumran, and therefore suggest that it may have served as a rest stop for travelers crossing the Dead Sea to the hot springs of Callirhoe on the opposite shore, even positing that it had port facilities at a time when the level of the Dead Sea was higher.

A water reservoir at Qumran

Another theory notes that Qumran's layout is very similar to manor houses owned by an absentee landlord and worked by hired labor. If Qumran was such a complex, what was its main product? One of the site's heretofore unexplained installations is precisely one of those used for the production of perfume, probably from the balsam plant. It is possible that the Essenes, whom Josephus describes as "excellent men, wholly given over to agricultural labor" (Antiquities 18:1:19) chose Qumran as a place where they could make their living while still pursuing the solitude and purity of desert life.

Overview of the Qumran complex

A Balsam Factory

Some scholars believe that this unusual structure at Qumran may have been part of a furnace that heated water to process the balsam plant.

The most famous pharmaceutical and cosmetic of the ancient Holy Land was balsam, mentioned in use already in Old Testament times (Genesis 37:25, Jeremiah 8:22, 51:8). Josephus calls it "an ointment of all the most precious" (Antiquities 14:4,1), and notes that it was produced near Jericho. Production of this expensive plant into medicine and cosmetics was kept such a secret that the plant, which has been identified with *commiphora opobalsamum* of ancient records, has become extinct.

Josephus reports that the balsam sap exuded "like tears" from its branches when they were cut with sharp stones (Wars of the Jews 1:6:6). Once in the factory, two forms of fragrance were manufactured: the sap was made directly into an unguent, *opus balsamun*, the most expensive form of the product. The other product was made when the branches of the plant were cooked in water in big baths. The resulting juices were mixed with olive oil. This product was called aromatic oil. In such a factory there would be furnaces and big vats of water.

This jar, with the word "balsam" written on it in Hebrew letters, was discovered at Masada and no doubt contained this precious commodity.

At work in the balsam factory

The Dead Sea Scrolls

Fragment of a daily prayer

The Dead Sea Scrolls were discovered in 1947 by a Bedouin goat herder in a cave above mysterious ruins at Qumran on the northwest shore of the lowest and saltiest body of water on earth that gave them their name. Since that day, the scrolls have mesmerized scholars and lay people alike. The reason is simple: they contain texts of the oldest Hebrew Bible ever discovered, predating by nearly one thousand years the next-known oldest Hebrew biblical manuscripts.

The discovery of the first seven scrolls was followed over the next decade by the discovery of another 200 scrolls and thousands of additional fragments. While the Isaiah Scroll was the only book discovered in its entirety, the scrolls comprise segments of every book of the Bible except Esther. Most of this scriptural treasure was discovered accidentally, years after the initial find, in a cave not far from where archaeologists were busy exploring the ancient ruins of Qumran.

With the notable exception of one scroll written on copper and containing an arcane description of hidden treasure, the scrolls were written mainly on parchment (a few were inscribed on papyrus) with carbon-based ink. Some scrolls were discovered wrapped in linen and placed in tall cylindrical jars, others seemed to have been placed hastily in the caverns, as if to hide them from prying eyes.

While scholarly debate refuses to rest on anything concerning the Dead Sea Scrolls, it now appears to some that the scrolls were written by different hands, and perhaps in different areas of the country, before being deposited in the caves.

Interior of a Qumran cave

Part of the Habbakuk Commentary

One of the clay jars in which the Qumran scrolls were discovered

What is in the Dead Sea Scrolls?

About 40% of the contents is similar to the masoretic text (masoretic means traditional, and is the name for the next oldest Hebrew text, contained in the Aleppo Codex and dating from the tenth century CE). Some of the scrolls are similar to the Septuagint, the Greek translation of the Bible from Hebrew written in the second century BCE, while yet other scrolls are similar to the ancient version of the Bible used by the Samaritans. Some scrolls are completely unique, such as certain previously unknown Psalms and an Aramaic book of Job and Leviticus.

Scroll fragment from Leviticus 26:2-16

Fragment of a Pentateuch scroll from Qumran, written in Paleo-Hebraic script

An inkpot discovered at Qumran. Remains of the carbon-based ink were discovered within.

Who Wrote the Scrolls?

In addition to Bible scrolls, other scrolls discovered at Qumran are known as the sectarian writings. These contain the beliefs of the people who called themselves *hayahad*, "the covenant".

The sectarian writings indicate that its members first left Jerusalem under the leadership of one they called Teacher of Righteousness, and during the term of office of an "evil priest", recognized variously as one of the many high priests that rose and fell from power, or perhaps one of the Hasmonean kings. The *yahad* accused the high priests of abuses of power and felt that worship in the Temple was not carried out in the requisite state of purity.

The group responded to these ills by leaving the cities to start a new, purer way of life in the desert. The group's writings show that belief in the End of Days was an important part of their faith. A time would come, they foretold, when the wicked would be destroyed during a great battle between the forces of good and evil, known to them as the "Children of Light" and the "Children of Darkness". Israel would then be liberated from the yoke of foreign domination. The survivors of the battle (the members of the sect), led by a righteous high priest, would bring a "great light to the world and light up the faces of many" (From the portion of the Community Rule scroll known as *Serach Habrachot*).

The group lived a communal life, eating, studying and praying together. They took all their decisions together, counseled by their elders. Great emphasis was placed on ritual purity, achieved by frequent immersion in a ritual bath.

As a means of separating themselves from other Jews, they did not sacrifice in the Temple and they maintained a solar calendar instead of the lunar one used by mainstream Judaism.

Most scholars agree that John the Baptist may have spent time studying and living with the people of Qumran and that his emphasis on water immersion may have had its origins in exposure to the teachings of the sect. Scholars also point to Essene terminology appearing in the New Testament, such as the words "children of light" (Luke 16:8, John 12:36, Ephesians 5:8, I Thes. 5:5), as hints of the teachings of the sect which filtered into early Christianity.

Part of an appendix to the Manual of Discipline, rule book of the Qumran Community

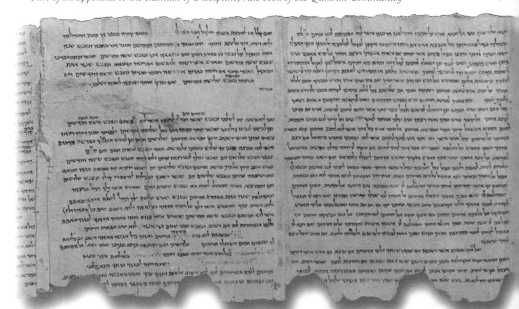

Sandal nails from Qumran

"They despise riches, in vain would one search for one with a greater fortune than another. All of them loving frugality and hating luxury as a plague for body and soul"(Philo, Apologia pro Judais 4)

"All are to dine together" (the Community Rule)

Numerous clay bowls and plates were discovered in the Qumran "pantry."

The Copper Scrolls, before opening

"Whatever they receive as salary is not kept to themselves but is deposited before them all" (Wars of the Jews 2:8:3)

A hoard of coins discovered at Qumran

A fragment of the famed Copper Scroll

"And you shall clean(se) all (by) our ho(ly) laws
And then he shall enter the water...
He will recite and say Blessed are
[you, God of Israel...] according to your command
[the cleansing of all] (things) is defined."
(From the Baptismal Liturgy of the Sect)

The ritual immersion bath at Qumran

Masada:
A Desert Fortress Like None Other

Herod knew when to call upon the protection of Masada. When his rival, the Hasmonean Antigonus, became part of a plot to unleash the Parthians on Judea and Herod's fortunes plummeted, it was to this lofty plateau-fortress that he dispatched his mother and sister, as well as Mariamne, his betrothed, his future mother-in-law and additional "wives and followers" numbering some 800, in order to ensure their safety.

But it was far more than an armed camp to which these noblewomen and their retinue were dispatched. In fact, rather than call Masada a fortress, scholars now prefer the word "fortified palace". Herod must have loved personally supervising Masada's construction. Though masons' marks in Hebrew show the workmen were local, the style suggests that these builders had trained in Rome or in the construction of some of the mansions in Pompeii.

Could Herod, consummate collaborator with Rome, ever have imagined the use to which his opulent palace would eventually be put ? In 66 CE, a Jewish political sect known as the Sicarii, extreme in their opposition to Rome, broke into Masada to obtain weapons stored there. Forced out of Jerusalem by their political opponents, the Sicarii continued their battles from Masada, remaining there even after the Temple lay in ruins and the war was all but over. But when the Romans finally

Artist's rendering of Masada in Herod's time

turned their attention to the insurgents, even Herod's massive fortifications could not help them. In the spring of 73 CE, Roman siege machines breached Masada's walls, only to discover that the Sicarii had taken their own lives and the lives of their families, rather than surrender to the hated conqueror.

The swimming pool

The storerooms

THE SWIMMING POOL

Herod's builders carved the building blocks for Masada's buildings from the mountain itself. Later, the quarries were used for various purposes, especially water storage. The size and shape of this pool rule out its use as either a ritual bath or a simple reservoir. The square niches in an adjacent wall reveal the recreational use of the pool — they were likely used for the storage of items of clothing belonging to bathers.

THE STOREROOMS

According to Josephus, the storerooms built by Herod contained all things necessary for a siege (Wars 7:8:4). The excavator, Prof. Yigael Yadin, reports the discovery of various types of vessels, oil, wine and flour jars, each with their own distinctive shape.

THE HOSTEL

This complex is of a type common throughout Europe in the Roman Imperial period. Such structures housed officials plying the famed Roman road system in the fulfillment of their duties. The complex, located near the eastern entrance gate of Masada, consisted of nine apartments grouped around an open-air courtyard and may have provided housing for members of Herod's entourage or other visitors to the fortress.

THE COLUMBARIUM

A round tower on the south side of Masada is believed to have been a dovecote. The raising of pigeons served many purposes in the herodian era, among them for sacrifice in the Temple, and for the use of their droppings for fertilizer. The columbarium tower at Masada could have had purely decorative purposes, with white doves flying to and fro adding another pleasing dimension to the lush garden that apparently graced the south sector of Masada.

The hostel

The columbarium

The Northern Palace

The Northern Palace

The northern palace, looking northeast

Perhaps the most magnificent edifice on Masada, the three-tiered northern palace served as the royal residence. The northern palace was located close to well-stocked storerooms and the luxuriously appointed bathhouse. A watchtower stood guard over this entire strategic end of the plateau, where soldiers no doubt remained on duty round the clock to protect both the royal personages when in residence, and their possessions.

The palace was separated from the rest of the complex by its own high protective wall, penetrated by a narrow corridor that led to the private apartments on the top level of the northern palace. These rooms were richly decorated with frescoes and one was graced with a window.

The middle level of the palace

The lowest level of the palace was a banquet hall. It was surrounded by engaged columns and fresco-covered walls. Between the columns were additional windows through which diners could enjoy the spectacular desertscape. A small bathhouse was also located at this level. In between, the middle level was a *tholos*, a circular structure that may have been used as a kind of conservatory-rest area.

Herod must have ordered his architects to seek out the coolest spot on this desert mountaintop for his personal quarters, for the northern palace is bathed in cool breezes that sweep down from nearby wadis every hour of the day, and especially in the evening. Open balconies on each level ensured maximum enjoyment of the best climate conditions on the plateau.

Lower level of the northern palace

In such pleasant surroundings, Herod's fiancée Mariamne, her mother and his mother would have passed an enforced retirement period during the precarious early days of his reign.

Years later, when Herod's power was at its zenith, he may have invited his friend Marcus Agrippa, son-in-law of his patron Augustus, to Masada. Standing on the balcony of the *tholos*, he probably basked in compliments he received on the design of his palace, so similar to Marcus Agrippa's own villa on the banks of the Tiber in Rome. From this vantage point, Herod could also show off his balsam groves, shimmering in the heat not far to the north at Ein Gedi, a major source of the wealth that allowed him to construct the extravagant wilderness showcase that was Masada.

Frescoes on the lower level of the palace

A Corinthian capital found on the lower terrace

The Bathhouse

This largest of Masada's bathhouses was adjacent to the northern palace and probably served the royal family and honored guests. Much of the material for the bathhouse, as well as the crew that constructed it, may have been imported from Italy, showing once again the care Herod took to precisely imitate Roman culture through its architecture.

A courtyard paved with a simple black and white mosaic served as the *palaestra* or exercise court associated with bathhouses. It led to a dressing room, or *apodyterium*, paved with unusual triangular tiles made of limestone and slate laid point to base. From the dressing room, bathers would pass through the cold water room to a rest area called the *tepidarium*, where they could enjoy a rubdown, and on to the steam room, the *caldarium*.

The steam room, whose vaulted roof was adorned with molded and painted plaster, was heated by a furnace above which a water reservoir was placed. The furnace was connected by lead pipes to a tub in the steam room itself. Heated air moved from the furnace into the space beneath a suspended floor and from there to hollow rectangular bricks that covered the walls. This system provided extra heat, as well as keeping the walls dry, as steam could not condense on the hot surface. The circulation of air also kept the wood-burning furnace going at full blast. Imprints of the tiles on the floor show it was richly decorated. Four chimneys released smoke and gases from the furnace to the outside.

The bathhouse, therefore, was far from merely a place to cleanse oneself; it was an aesthetic experience, a cultural institution, of which the steam room, regardless of the weather outside (which at Masada must have been stiflingly hot most of the year) was an inseparable part. Here one could pass time with friends and gauge the power of adversaries. No doubt numerous lucrative business deals and more than one plot were hatched in the aromatic vapors of Masada's bathhouse.

Pastime of the Rich and Famous

Men usually visited the baths in the afternoon, while women went during the less popular morning hours. A variety of fragrant oils were applied during the massage that was an essential part of the bathhouse experience. Soap was a paste made from the fruit of the lupine plant. After the bath, both the person and his or her clothes would be anointed with fragrant oil from plants like crocus, myrtle and cypress, or the costly nard.

In the wealthy country estates of Italy, baths have often been discovered adjacent to the estate kitchen, sharing its stove as a heat source. It is possible that these facilities, cramped in comparison with the Masada bathhouse and other similar complexes, were used by slaves and servants, because the larger baths were mainly reserved for the wealthy. In excavations of what have been defined as "tenements"—lower class ancient homes in Rome, no bathing facilities at all have been discovered.

This bath was built against a wall of the dressing room after Herod's time.

Columns supporting the floor of the steam room

Water for the bathhouse and other needs was stored in cisterns like this, hewed from the solid rock. They were fed by aqueducts leading from wadis (dry riverbeds) whose water came from flash floods.

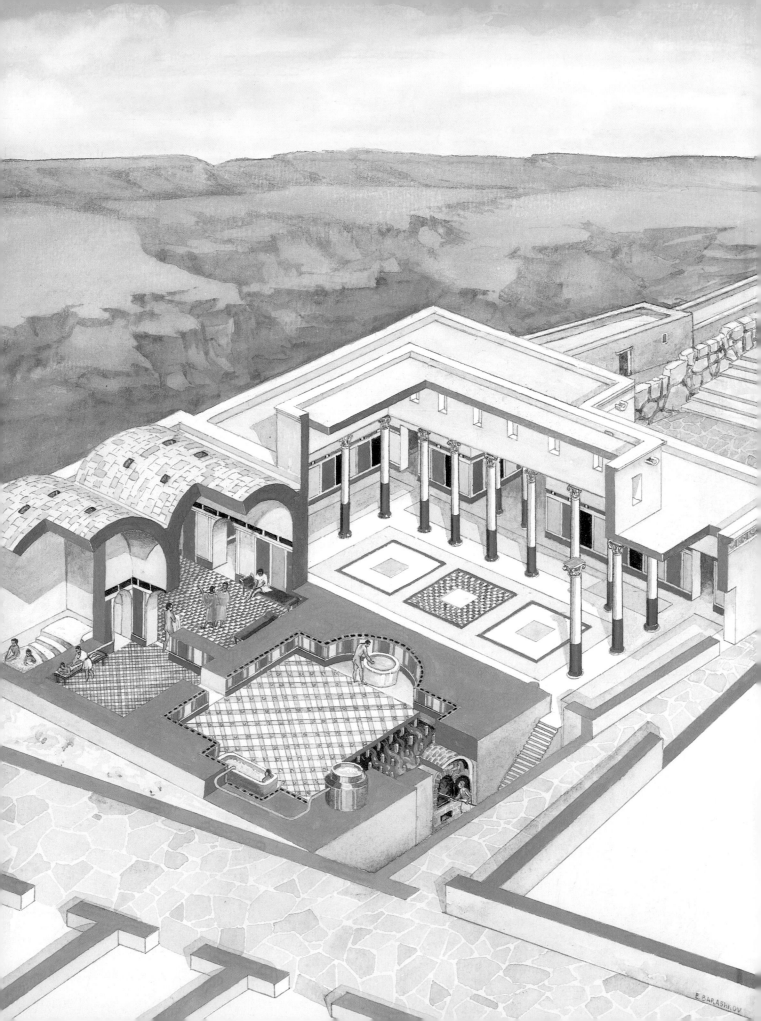

The Western Palace

If Masada's northern palace was Herod's home at Masada, then the open and reception areas, baths, kitchens and guardhouse wing of the western palace, all surrounding a central courtyard, indicate that this opulent building was his "business address". One of the rooms had four depressions in the floor, which Masada excavator Yigael Yadin interpreted as devices to hold posts that supported a canopy over a throne. Walls may have been concealed with wall-hangings, which archaeologists have identified as a thick layer of ash containing charred ropes and bronze rings. A second story of the western palace may have contained guest apartments and viewing terraces for the pleasure of visitors.

In the western palace bathhouse, a mosaic common to others of the time combines bands of differing widths but of the same color, with other designs.

Mosaic from the western palace bathhouse

The Mosaic Artist

Mosaic floors were a common decoration for wealthy homes and public places in ancient Rome. Their appearance in Judea around the time of Herod is clear testimony of the cultural and economic allegiance to Rome established by his father and furthered by himself. In a city like Caesarea, the work of the mosaic masters would have been much in demand.

Josephus records that Herod "...imitated everything, though ever so costly or magnificent, in other nations". Herodian mosaics are characterized by black and white patterns as well as plain, colored bands interspersed with the more complex designs that served to emphasize them. Among the designs are the serrated saw-tooth and a wave pattern thought to come from the hellenistic world of the sea. Vine leaves, pomegranates and grapes are unusual. Simple vine scroll is more common; the addition of the fruits may be some of the fruits of the land of Israel which were among the earliest motifs in Jewish art. Rosettes, which appear often on stone carvings as well, are a more common design than any other.

In the Roman world outside Judea, mosaics abounded in elaborate human and animal figures. But of all the herodian-era mosaics discovered in Herod's palaces at Masada, Jericho, Herodium and Cypros, not one contains human or animal figures.

The reason for this is clear. Herod was well aware that imitating the human and animal images of the non-Jewish artistic world would anger his Jewish subjects, as they contravened the Second Commandment. Such flouting of Jewish ritual, even by the king, contained the potential for violence that would disrupt the smooth running of his kingdom and bring the wrath of Rome upon him. It is therefore more than a nod towards Jewish tradition that Herod chose as a motif for this mosaic some of the "seven fruits" of the land of Israel mentioned in Deuteronomy 8:8.

The stones, or tesserae, were cut with a hammer and chisel, mainly from limestone containing the desired hues, iron oxide for red and magnesium for green and black. Large, naturally flat stones were laid out to even out the work space, on top of which lime-and-ash mortar was spread. While still wet, the mortar was incised by the mosaic master with the parallel lines between which the design would appear. Sometimes, the design was painted onto the cement before the stones were laid by his apprentices.

Mosaic from the western palace bathhouse

Herod's Other Palaces

Herod, the Great Builder

Jericho

The golden age of Herod's rule included the construction of Caesarea with its port, one of the largest ports in the Mediterranean. He rebuilt and expanded the ancient capital at Samaria and expanded the old Greek town. Both Caesarea and Sebastea were named for Herod's patron, formerly Octavian, now called Augustus, the August One (Sebaste in Greek). Both cities, as well as the town of Paneas (later Caesarea Philipi), contained huge temples to his patron.

Among some fifteen other building projects was the second largest palace in the world, at Herodion. But the complex for which he is perhaps most famous, the largest building project of the Roman world of its time, was the Jerusalem Temple. Built on the selfsame site where the First Temple had stood, which was on the site where David had purchased a threshing floor from Ornan the Jebusite, the Temple was the symbol of the presence of the spirit of God among the people.

Machaerus

It was also the symbol of everything that was enigmatic about this despotic ruler, right down to the gigantic golden eagle that he ordered placed over the Temple gate. He purchased a thousand robes for the priests, but the garments of the high priest, to the latter's chagrin, he kept in the Antonia Fortress, allowing them to be worn only on the holy days, after which they would be returned to his keeping. During a famine, he once remitted a third of the taxes he collected to the people. But those same citizens were not permitted to meet, walk, or eat together, says Josephus. Herod "watched everything they did, and when any were caught, they were severely punished and many there were who were brought to the citadel Hyrcania, both openly and secretly, and were there put to death. And there were spies sent everywhere, both in the cities and on the roads...and for those who could in no way be reduced to acquiesce...he persecuted them all manner of ways" (Antiquities of the Jews 15:366-368). Herod earned his epithet "the great" as a builder, while sorely lacking other virtues.

Sartaba (Alexandrion)

Hyrcania

Herodion

Caesarea

Herod built cities like Jerusalem and Caesarea Maritima in the style of the great gentile cities he had known, though not as elaborate. He intended them to be inhabited by his Jewish subjects and in constructing them, he strengthened the status of the Jewish communities in these places and also that of his own ethnic community, the Idumeans.

Herod built Caesarea on a site that had been settled centuries before by Phoenician seafarers and had been known as Strato's Tower. When Augustus awarded him the area, Herod decided to turn Strato's Tower into his main seaport. As his son Philip would later do at Paneas (Caesarea Philipi) he named the city in honor of his patron, Augustus Caesar. The port Herod designated Sebastos, the second time he honored Augustus by naming a place for him using the Greek form of his title.

It took Herod twelve years to build the city. Like his other cities, Caesarea had two major focal points: the temple and the palace. Its underground drainage system was very elaborate and almost as beautiful, Josephus says, as the buildings above ground. The city boasted magnificent public structures, including a theater and a stadium where Herod initiated games that took place every fifth year and became world-famous. Water needs for the city's some 15,000 residents were supplied by an aqueduct that transported water from springs in the foothills of the Carmel range to the east, tunneling, where necessary, about 1200 feet. The industrial zone of the city, containing any workshops that would emit noxious fumes (like the tanner's

"But Festus answered that Paul should be kept at Caesarea, and that he himself was going there shortly. Therefore "he said "let those who have authority among you go down with me and accuse this man, to see if there is any fault in him."

(Acts 25: 4-5)

Inscription mentioning the name of Pontius Pilate and a temple he dedicated to Tiberius in Caesarea

| Herod's harbour | The Crusader tower | Modern port | Aqueduct | East gate | Promontory palace | Herod's amphitheater | Cardo Maximus | Roman theater |

The ruins of Caesarea as seen today

The northern aqueduct

workshop) or noise of carts or machinery, was situated to the east, so that prevailing winds would carry the smells away from the town. Rome's procurators established themselves at Caesarea and probably lived in the palace that Herod had built in his day, in the wake of the chaotic reign of his son Archelaus when the Romans restored direct rule to the country.

In this context, we meet Caesarea in the New Testament. It was the home of the Centurion Cornelius, the first Gentile convert to Christianity. King Agrippa I met his unpleasant death here. Later, Paul the Apostle was brought to the city as a prisoner and appeared before the procurators Felix and Festus and finally before King Agrippa II, after which he left from the Caesarea port for Rome to set his case before Caesar.

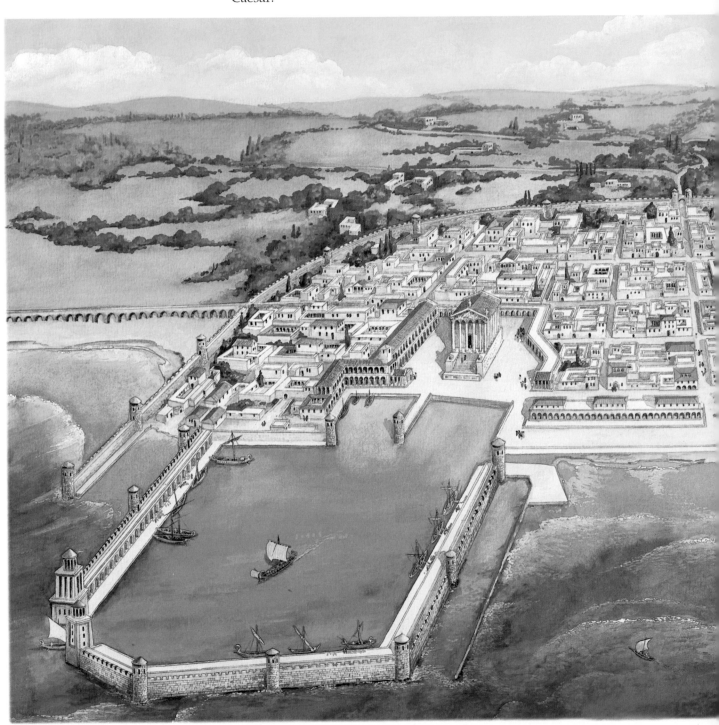

It was in Caesarea that, in 66 CE, the Great Revolt of the Jews against the Romans actually broke out when inter-communal strife between Jews and Greeks set off a riot, the shock waves of which emanated through the entire country. During the years of the revolt, Vespasian was quartered in the city. As a consequence of the revolt, the city lost its royal status and like the rest of the country, went into decline. In 79 CE, the cataclysmic eruption of Mount Vesuvius in Italy brought Tsunami waves to the shores of the Holy Land, laying waste to much of the town. Thus, by the end of the first century CE, much of the city had sunk back into the sand.

This statue may have stood in one of Caesarea's pagan shrines.

The walled city of Caesarea. In Herod's day the population of Caesarea reached about 15,000.

The theater

The amphitheater

The Port of Caesarea

"And when he had landed at Caesarea, and gone up and greeted the church, he went down to Antioch." (Acts 18:22)

Herod's port in Caesarea was the largest in the eastern Mediterranean and one of the busiest, exporting all the riches of the east to Rome, only a ten day journey away.

The port consisted of an outer basin protected by two artificial sea walls. The southern breakwater was 1800 feet long and over 160 feet wide. At the tip of the southern breakwater was a huge lighthouse tower, which Herod named for Drusus, Augustus' son-in-law who had died young.

It was from this port that Paul the Apostle set sail for Rome (Acts 27:1).

The sea walls were constructed out of huge blocks, each one some 12 feet high by 52 feet long and 21 feet wide, created by pouring concrete into wooden forms. The concrete utilized an important new building material, volcanic ash instead of sand. The concrete was poured and hardened under water, the first use of hydraulic concrete anywhere in the world. A sluice system kept the port free of silt.

Opposite page:
A lighthouse is presumed to be one of the towers marking the entrance to the protected inner port of Caesarea.

The southern breakwater of Herod's port lies beneath these modern and Crusader structures.

A Pagan Temple

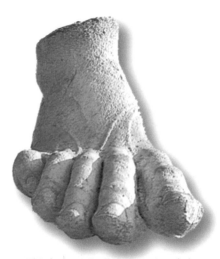

This fragment is all that remains of the monumental statue of a god or emperor that once stood in Caesarea

Steps leading to the temple Herod built for Augustus in Sebastea

"...a temple was seen a great way off by those sailing for that haven, and had in it two statues, the one of Rome, and the other of Caesar."
(Antiquities 15:9:6)

The term "god" had an entirely different meaning to pagans than to Jews and Christians. For Jews and Christians, God is the all-powerful creator of the universe and everything within it. Pagans, on the other hand, saw their deities as the highest of three species of beings. The relations between the species were somewhat of a "sliding scale". Caligula could make his horse a senator and Augustus and other rulers could become gods merely by moving up the scale that began with animals and ended with the gods.

Pagans made offerings to the god of their choice in expectation of initiating a contract that would be honored in the same manner as a contract between humans. Visiting the temple was part of paying homage to the deity. That was the time when, to effect compliance with the contract, the god would be worn down with prayers, much as a merchant would wear down a potential customer in any way he could, including with gifts and vows, in an effort to sell his goods. The deity, therefore, was considered a patron and a friend who could be influenced.

Judeo-Christian faith in God as the Almighty Father presents a powerful contrast to the pagan view of religion. In the words of Jesus, "For your Father knows the things you have need of before you ask Him" (Matt 6:7-8).

The space dedicated to the pagan deity began as a simple square enclosure. This form of architecture dated from the early days of Roman religion when augurs, priests whose task it was to tell the future, were required to divide the space where they practiced into equal-sized quadrants correspondng to the points on the compass. Later, as temples became more elaborate, they contained a statue of the deity to which they were dedicated in a raised area accessed by steps. A colonnaded outer porch served as a gathering place for supplicants, as only priests were allowed to enter the temple's inner sanctum. Temples were constructed either on high places or on raised platforms to increase the impression they made. Some Roman temples had as many as six stepped terraces before the inner sanctum was reached. An altar for offerings sometimes stood at the base of the steps.

The City Gate and Market

"...for no one buys their merchandise anymore: merchandise of gold and silver, precious stones and pearls, fine linen and purple, silk and scarlet, every kind of citron wood, every kind of object of ivory, every kind of object of most precious wood, bronze, iron, and marble; and cinnamon and incense, fragrant oil and frankincense, wine and oil, fine flour and wheat, cattle and sheep, horses and chariots, and bodies and souls of men." (Rev 18:11-13)

The city gate was a bustling place. In its spacious inner court, the *agoranomos* had his tax station where salt and various types of produce would be weighed and the customs owed on it would be calculated and paid. A money changer's booth was on hand as well.

Passersby would pause in the inner court of the gate to play games of chance. Pedestrians, litter bearers and pack animals vied for space, but due to a law enacted throughout the empire in the days of emperor Marcus Aurelius, no wagons or other vehicular traffic were allowed in the city during the daylight hours.

Soldiers were on duty at the top of the 36 foot-high towers and the tops of the 24 foot-high crenellated walls. At night, they would close the enormous wooden gates, which would be reopened only at dawn. The wooden gates had a small opening that allowed passage after the identity of the person without had been ascertained, even when the gate itself was closed. This is probably the type of gate Jesus referred to when he said: "Enter by the narrow gate: for wide is the gate, and broad is the way, that leads to destruction, and there are many who go in: Because narrow is the gate, and difficult is the way which leads to life, and there are few who find it" (Matt 7:13-14).

A contemporary market scene

This arch was part of the northern gateway to the walled city of Jerusalem in the late Roman era. Deep grooves discovered in the upper part of the gate were probably made by the saddles of camels heavily laden with merchandise as they passed through the gate on their way to the city market.

Spices and other commodities from around the world were hawked in the markets of big cities such as Caesarea.

Currency and Prices

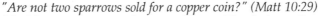

The pruta, or mite

The pruta, or mite

The earliest form of the pruta was minted by Alexander Janaeus (103-76 BCE). This copper coin was the smallest unit of currency, and was equal to the Roman quadrans. There were 192 prutot to the dinar. Archaeological evidence has uncovered tens of thousands of these tiny copper coins, showing that it was by far the most common coin in circulation in antiquity and continued to be used until the fourth century CE.

"Are not two sparrows sold for a copper coin?" (Matt 10:29)
"And he saw also a certain poor widow putting in two mites." (Luke 21:2)
"Assuredly I say to you, some will by no means get out of there till you have paid the last penny." (Matt 5:26)

A mite from the time of Alexander Janaeus

The silver dinar

The silver dinar

The most common silver dinar at the time of Jesus had the name of Tiberius on one side, and on the other side showed a seated female figure with the words "High Priest", another of the emperor's titles. Most of these coins were minted in Caesarea in Cappadocia.

"Show me a denarius. Whose image and inscription does it have?" They answered and said, "Caesar's". (Luke 20:24)
"Or what woman, having ten silver coins, if she loses one coin, does not light a lamp, sweep the house, and search carefully until she finds it?" (Luke 15:8)
"On the next day, when he departed, he took out two denarii, gave them to the innkeeper, and said to him, "Take care of him; and whatever more you spend, when I come again, I will repay you." (Luke 10:35)

A silver dinar from the time of Tiberius

The Tyrian shekel:

The Tyrian shekel

The Tyrian shekel had a silver weight of about 14.2 grams of silver. This coin, minted between 126 BCE and 56 CE, was considered of dependable value and therefore it was used for payment of the Temple tax. It was worth four dinars, double the amount of an ordinary shekel. The task of the moneychangers (John 2:13-16, Matt 21:12-13, Mark 11:15) in the Temple was to change other forms of currency into the Tyrian coinage for those paying the Temple tax. Not all Tyrian shekels were necessarily minted in Tyre. In fact, after the time of Augustus, the minting of Tyrian coins in Tyre stopped. But since payment of the Temple tax was still required in this pure silver, Herod began to mint his own silver coins. "What is a Tyrian silver coin?", asks the Tosefta (*Ketuboth* 13:20). "It is a Jerusalemite".

"Nevertheless, lest we offend them, go to the sea, cast in a hook, and take the fish that comes up first. And when you have opened its mouth, you will find a piece of money; take that and give it to them for Me and you." (Matt 17:24)

The shekel of the Jewish Revolt

The shekel of the Jewish Revolt

The right to mint coins was accorded by sovereign nations. Therefore, when the Great Revolt broke out, as a sign of independence from Rome, the revolutionaries began to mint their own coins. The coins bear Hebrew inscriptions in archaic Hebrew script and Jewish symbols, an important innovation, as even coins minted by Jewish governors prior to the revolt contained no Jewish symbols. Coins were struck from the first to the fifth and last year of the Great Revolt. These coins serve as poignant guides to archaeologists excavating sites from that era as the year of the latest coin discovered tells how long the revolutionaries were able to hold out in a specific place.

What would a Shekel buy ?

In spite of the difficulties which arise in determining the exact cost of items during the lifetime of Jesus, it is interesting to look at prices as they appear in ancient texts, including the Mishnah, the New Testament, and rarely, archaeological discoveries. Food, as we can see, was relatively inexpensive. We can understand this against the background of life in the days of Jesus, when most people were farmers who manufactured almost all of the goods needed in their daily lives within the family circle.

A great deal of confusion arises over the use of various terms denoting the same coin. For example, the word "dinar", used in the price list below, is the Hebrew or Aramaic form of the Latin word denarius, and would have probably been the word Jesus used. In Greek, the denarius is called a drachma. Shekel is a Hebrew word first found in Genesis 24:22 and occurring often in the Old Testament. Two dinars were equal to one shekel, and four dinars to the more greatly valued Tyrian shekel.

Vineyard worker:
Daily wage: 1 dinar

A scribe's salary:
12 dinars a week

1 kor (220 liters)
of wheat:
1 gold aurelius
(25 silver dinars)

Cloak of a rich man:
100-200 dinars

Tallit (outer cloak) :
12 dinars

Price for weaving
a tallit:
8 dinars

A large meal:
1 dinar

1 seah
(about 2 gallons)
of flour: 1 dinar

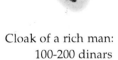

Loaf of bread:
1/12 dinar

1 amphora
of olive oil:
1 dinar

Pomegranate:
1 prutah

Cluster
of grapes:
1 prutah

Ram:
8 dinars

Lamb:
4 dinars

Calf:
20 dinars

Ox:
100-200 dinars

A newborn
donkey foal:
2-4 dinars

Rental
of a house
for a month:
4 dinars

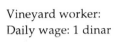

Bride-price
for a virgin:
200 dinars
(a widow, 100 dinars)

A woman's yearly
clothing allowance
from her husband:
50 dinars

A Roman soldier's
salary for a year:
50 dinars

By mid-first century CE, the price of two pigeons had skyrocketed to one gold dinar (equal to 25 silver dinars), a price far beyond the means of the simple people who would purchase them to offer in the Jerusalem Temple. Eventually, the sages imposed a price ceiling on this most common of sacrifices.

Bibliography

Adan-Bayewitz, David. Common Pottery in Roman Galilee. Ramat Gan: Bar Ilan University Press, 1993.

Ariel, Yisrael. The Odyssey of the Third Temple. Jerusalem: G. Israel Publications and Productions, 1993.

Avigad, Nahman. The Herodian Quarter in Jerusalem. Jerusalem: Keter, 1989.

Avitzor, Shmuel. Man and His Work, Historical Atlas of Tools and Workshops in the Holy Land. Jerusalem: Carta and the Israel Exploration Society, 1976.

Avni, Gideon and Zvi Greenhut. "The Alkedama Tombs." Israel Antiquities Authority Reports, Volume 1 (1996).

The Babylonian Talmud CD Rom edition, Otzrot Yisrael, Bar Ilan University.

Beer, Moshe. "The Attitude of the Sages Towards Riding Horses." Cathedra (Journal for the History of the Land of Israel) Volume 60 (June 1991).

The Bible, The New King James Version, CD-Rom Edition, Biblesoft, 1992-1998

Bivin, David. "The Hem of His Garment". Jerusalem Perspective, April 1988.

Connolly, Peter. Pompeii. London: Macdonald Educational, 1979.

Carcopuno, Jerome. Daily Life in Ancient Rome. London: Peregrine Books, 1975.

Dar, Shimon, Yigal Tepper, and Zeev Safrai. Umm Reichan, Tel Aviv: Society for the Protection of Nature in Israel and Hakibbutz HaMeuhad, 1986.

Davies, Roy. Service in the Roman Army. Edinburgh: Edinburgh Univeristy Press, 1989.

Edwards, John. The Roman Cookery of Apicus. London: Random House, 1993.

The Encyclopedia Judaica, CD-ROM Edition, Jerusalem: Keter, 1997.

Foerster, Gideon, Masada V, Art and Architecture. Jerusalem: The Israel Exploration Society, 1995.

Goodman, Martin. The Ruling Class of Judaea. Cambridge: Cambridge University Press, 1995.

Grossberg, Asher "Ritual Preparation and Maintenance of Mikvaot at the Time of the Second Temple - Masada and Jerusalem." Abstract from Judea and Samaria Research Studies, Proceedings of the Seventh Annual Meeting, edited by Y. Eshel, 1997.

Guhl, E., and Koner, W. The Greeks and Romans, Their Life and Customs. London: Bracken Books, 1989.

Guri-Rimon, Ofra. "Treasure Houses and Administrative Centers: The Primary Purpose of the Desert Strongholds." Cathedra Vol. 82 (December. 1996).

Gutman, Shmarya. Gamla, A City in Rebellion. Tel Aviv: Ministry of Defense Publications, 1994.

Hachlili, Rachel. Ancient Jewish Art and Archaeology in the Land of Israel. New York: E.J. Brill, 1988.

Haaretz Museum. Vessels from the Period of the Mishna and the Talmud. Tel Aviv: Haaretz Museum, 1978.

Hendin, David. Guide to Biblical Coins. New York: Amphora Books, 1996.

Hirschfeld, Yizhar. The Palestinian Dwelling in the Roman-Byzantine Period. Jerusalem: Franciscan Printing Press and the Israel Exploration Society, 1995.

Hirschfeld, Yizhar. "Early Roman Manor Houses in Judea and the Site of Khirbet Qumran." Journal of Near Eastern Studies, Vol. 57, no. 3 (1998).

Nun, Mendel. The Sea of Galilee and its Fishermen in the New Testament. Jerusalem: Kibbutz Ein Gev Tourist Department and Kinneret Sailing Co., 1989.

Holum, Kenneth, Robert Hohlfelder, Robert J. Bull, and Avner Raban. King Herod's Dream, Caesarea on the Sea. New York W.W. Norton, 1988.

Hope, Thomas. Costumes of the Greeks and Romans. New York Dover Publications, 1962.

Humphrey, J.H., ed. "The Roman and Byzantine Near East, Some Recent Archaeological Research." Journal of Roman Archaeology, Supplementary Series, Number 14, 1995.

Levine, Lee I. "From Community Center to Lesser Sanctuary, the Furnishings and Interiors of the Ancient Synagogue." Cathedra No. 60, (June 1991).

Macaulay, David. City, A Story of Roman Planning and Construction. Boston: Houghtoon Mifflin, 1974.

Magen, Itzhak, "Jerusalem as a Center of Stone Production in the Days of Herod." Qadmoniot (Quartery for the Antiquities of the Land of Israel and Bible Lands). Vol 17 no 4, (1984).

Montefiori, C.G., and Loewe, H. A Rabbinic Commentary. New York: Schocken Books, 1974.

Van Der Vliet, N. "Sainte Marie Ou Elle Est Née" Et La Piscine Probatique, Jerusalem: Fransiscan Printing Press, 1938.

Netzer, Ehud. Herodion, Guide to the Site. Jerusalem: Herodion Archaeological Expedition.

Oppenheimer, A, Gafni, Y, Stern, M, eds. Jews and Judaism in the Second Temple, the Mishna and Talmud Period. Jerusalem: Yad Izhak Ben Zvi, 1993.

Perowne, Stuart. The Life and Times of Herod the Great, London: Hodder and Stoughton, 1963.

Reich, Ronny. "Six Stone Water Jars". Jerusalem Perspective, July-September, 1995.

Reich, Ronny. "Design and Maintenance of First Century Ritual Immersion Baths." Jerusalem Perspective, July-September 1999.

Rosovsky, Murray, ed. Illness and Healing in Ancient Times. Haifa: The Reuben and Edith Hecht Museum, 1997.

Safrai, Shmuel , "Did Jesus Wear a Kippa." Jerusalem Perspective, January-February 1992.

Safrai, Shmuel. "Synagogue and Sabbath" Jerusalem Perspective, November-December, 1989.

Safrai, Shmuel. The Second Temple and Mishna Periods, Studies in Society and Culture. Jerusalem: Ministry of Education, Zalman Shazar Center, 1983.

Safrai, Shmuel. "Shmuel Safrai Responds." Jerusalem Perspective, September-December 1994.

Safrai, Shmuel, "Jesus and the Hasidim." Jerusalem Perspective, January -June 1994.

Schechter, Erik. "The Thin Blue Line". The Jerusalem Report, May 10, 1999.

Sebesta, Judith Lynn, and Bonfante, Larissa, eds. The World of Roman Costume. Madison: University of Wisconsin Press, 1994.

Shatzman, Israel, The Armies of the Hasmonaeans and Herod. Tubingen: Mohr Publications, 1991.

Shiller, Eli, ed., Zeev Vilnay Book,   Essays on the history,

archaeology and lore of the Holy Land, Part II. Jerusalem: Ariel Books, 1987.

Sperber, Daniel. Roman Palestine 200-400, Money and Prices. Ramat Gan: Bar Ilan University, 1991.

Sperber, Daniel, Material Culture in Eretz Israel during the Talmudic Period. Jerusalem: Yad Itzhak Ben Zvi Press, Bar-Ilan University, 1993.

Steinzaltz, Adin. The Talmud, A Reference Guide. New York: Random House, 1989.

Veyne Paul, ed. A History of Private Life From Pagan Rome to Byzantium. Cambridge: Harvard University Press, 1987.

Whiston, William, trans, The Works of Josephus. USA: Hendrickson Publishers, 1995.

Wilson, Marvin, "The Appearance of Jesus." Jerusalem Perspective, November-December 1993.

Yadin, Yigael. Masada: Herod's Fortress and the Zealots' Last Stand. London: George Weidenfeld and Nicolson, 1966.

Young, Brad. The Parables, Jewish Tradition and Christian Interpretation. Peabody, Mass: Hendrickson Publishers, 1998.

Zias, Joe. "The Crucified Man from Giv'at Hamivtar: a Reappraisal." Israel Exploration Journal Vol. 35, No 1, 1985.

Zisu, Boaz. Tombs and Burials in Jerusalem in the Second Temple Period, New Discoveries 1980-1996, Masters Thesis. Jerusalem: The Hebrew University Institute of Archaeology, 1995.

From King David to Jesus

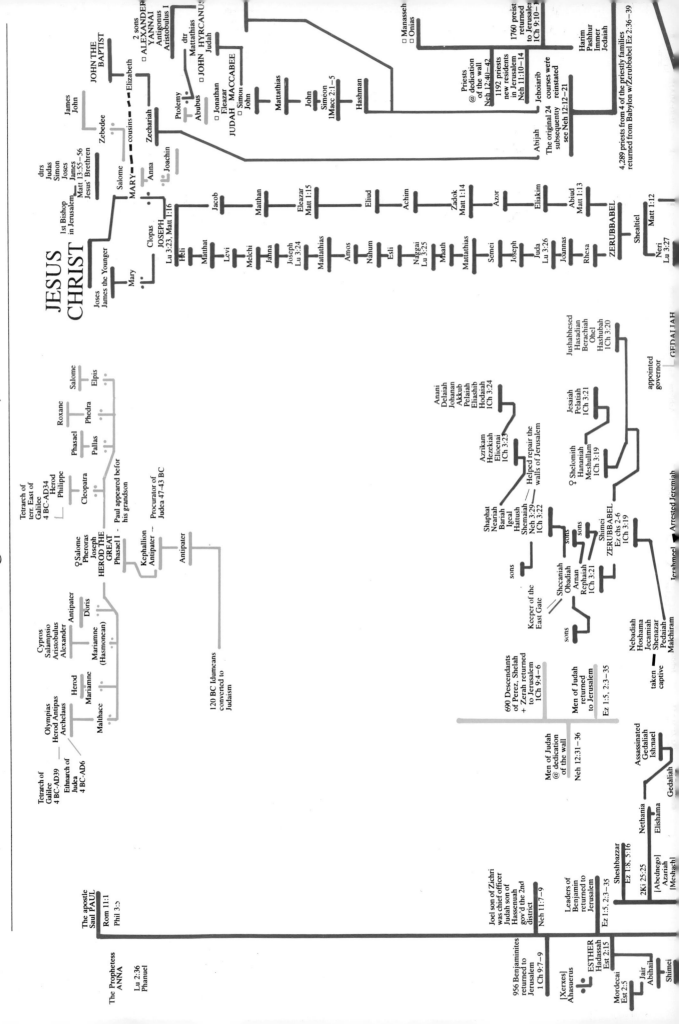

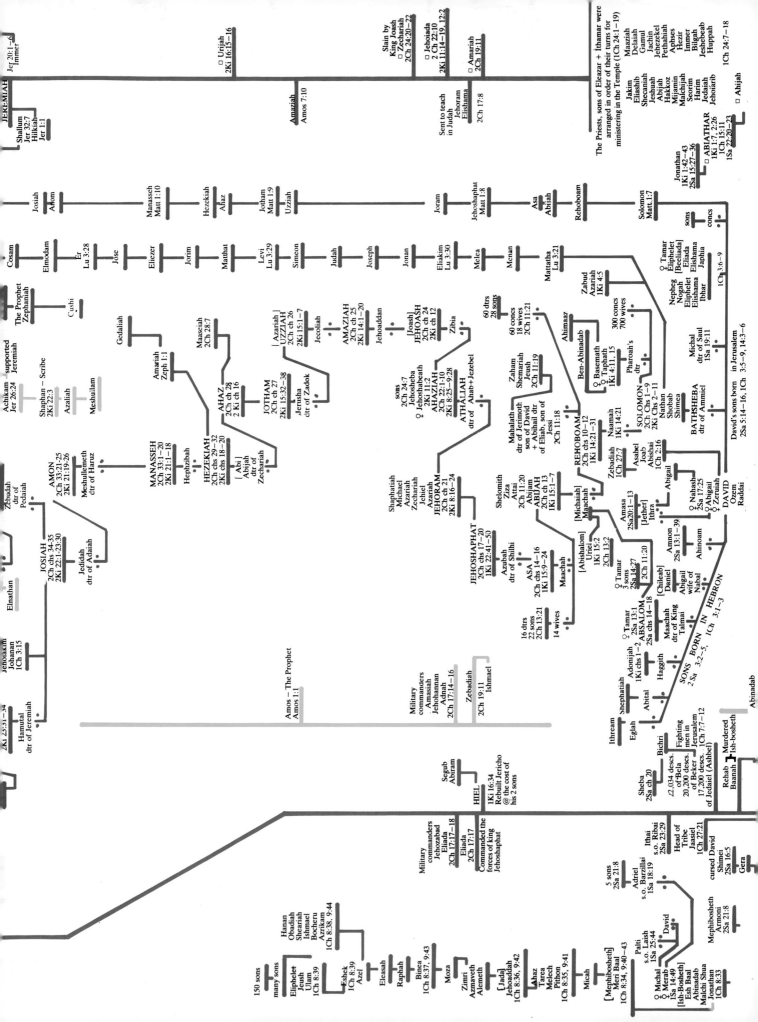

Index